"When I was creating the Rainforest Café, I sought to create a differentiated diner experience. In *Sales Differentiation*, Lee Salz provides you with the strategies to create a differentiated experience for your clientele. Salespeople often forget they have an opportunity to deliver meaningful value, not just with what they sell, but how they sell. Through great stories and anecdotes, this book teaches you how to do just that. I highly recommend it for anyone in sales."

—**STEVEN SCHUSSLER**, creator and founder of
Rainforest Café, T-REX, Yak & Yeti, and The Boathouse,
all featured at Walt Disney World in Orlando, Florida

"As a fan of Lee's work, I was excited to read his latest book. He delivers as usual! With *Sales Differentiation*, Lee provides the reader with an easy-to-understand primer for sales success. Written in a no-nonsense style, the book is filled with great examples. It is perfect for both beginning salespeople looking to develop their skills and experienced salespeople seeking to take their sales results to the next level. I will be recommending *Sales Differentiation* to my sales students!"

—**DAWN DEETER-SCHMELZ**, Ph.D., director, Kansas State University
National Strategic Selling Institute

"Here's the path to no longer hear the price objection ever again, as well as rendering your competitors as irrelevant. Lee Salz, in *Sales Differentiation*, shares his decades of real world sales success so all can now reap the rewards. Don't read this book—DEVOUR it!"

—**JACK DALY**, CEO/entrepreneur/coach
and best-selling business author

"I. Love. Everything. About. This. Book. Lee Salz not only powerfully describes why DIFFERENTIATION is so critical, but he shows you exactly how to differentiate yourself, your sales approach, and your messaging. Implementing the concepts in *Sales Differentiation* will get you more meetings with the right buyers, elevate how they view you and your solution, and help you close more business."

—**MIKE WEINBERG**, author of the *New Sales. Simplified.*
and *Sales Management. Simplified.*

"Sales organizations prosper when they eliminate the default activity of lowering prices to win sales. This will give you the knowledge and confidence to do just that."

—**TOM HOPKINS**, author of *When Buyers Say No*

"Lee Salz is the E. F. Hutton of customer acquisition. When Lee speaks, you should listen. In an over-crowded, over supplied world, Lee's insights into differentiating yourself by how you sell ring fresh and true. I regularly refer my clients to Lee and wait for the accolades to come streaming in— which they always do. Lee Salz's methods are practical and they work!"

—**BILL MILLS**, CEO, Executive Group, Inc.

"Everyone agrees that sales differentiation is a good thing, but no one has ever explained exactly what, why, and how to truly become differentiated. Until now. *Sales Differentiation* is a comprehensive and compelling look at an often-overlooked strategy for sales success."

—**DEB CALVERT**, author of *Stop Selling & Start Leading* and *DISCOVER Questions*®

"Finally, a definitive approach on what it means to differentiate yourself and what you sell. Lee Salz has done a masterful job of detailing multiple strategies you can use now to genuinely set yourself apart in the eyes of your customers. The value in the book is in his examples, which allow you to understand what you need to do to create a sales differential your customers will notice and, more importantly, pay for! This isn't a book to simply read. It's a book to read *and* apply. You won't regret it!"

—**MARK HUNTER**, CSP, "The Sales Hunter," author of *High-Profit Prospecting*

"*Sales Differentiation* shows how salespeople are more important than ever in terms of adding value and differentiating their product or service from the competition. The concepts presented by Lee Salz will help you in every phase of the sales process—from opening doors to winning deals at the prices you want. Make sure you have a pen, paper, and highlighter in hand when you read this book."

—**PAUL NOLAN**, editor, *Sales & Marketing Management* magazine

"Filled with dozens of proven concepts as well as highly-relatable stories, this book shows that salespeople who differentiate themselves not only win more deals, but they also win at higher margins. It is a brilliant and practical how-to guide for salespeople at every level. If you want to escape the high penalty that comes from the buyer's perception of sameness, this book is your key to success."

—**GERHARD GSCHWANDTNER**, CEO, *Selling Power* magazine

"Finally, a book that addresses differentiation in a step by step manner that allows salespeople to apply what they learn immediately. The practical easy-to-read format and examples to drive the point home are exceptional. Get this book in the hands of every salesperson you know."

—**ALICE HEIMAN**, founder and CSO
at Alice Heiman, LLC

"In today's sales environment where buyers are subjected to more sales 'noise' than ever, *Sales Differentiation* is a must-read (and must-implement) for any salesperson who wants to stand out and excel. With Lee's engaging, entertaining writing style, peppered with numerous stories and examples, you'll find yourself reading the book quickly. But, you'll want to go through it again several times to absorb, highlight, and write down the many valuable how-to's to use on your own calls."

—**ART SOBCZAK**, author of *Smart Calling*

"In *Sales Differentiation*, Lee delivers a fine addition to his line of outstanding sales reference tools. It's straightforward, packed full of real-world examples, and presented in a fresh, unique way as only Lee can. He not only addresses many common sales myths and barriers but provides examples and detailed processes to help you differentiate your products and services in a way that will catch a buyer's attention."

—**LARRY REEVES**, CEO, American Association
of Inside Sales Professionals

"In a sea of businesses and salespeople competing in the same spaces for the same dollars, being different is the only way to get an edge on your competition. Lee Salz has penned a fantastic and strategic book that gives salespeople the formula to do just that. Simply put, this book is not only incredibly useful, it's different."

—**KEN KUPCHIK**, author of *The Sales Survival Handbook*
and creator of Sales Humor

"If you want to compel your dream clients to change, you have to be different in a way that makes a difference. Lee Salz has written a comprehensive guide to differentiating your offering in a crowded, me-too marketplace. More importantly, this book will help you do the critical work of differentiating yourself!"

—**ANTHONY IANNARINO**, author of *Eat Their Lunch:*
Winning Clients Away from Your Competitors

"As I've traveled around the world over the past several years working with companies and their salespeople, I've been amazed to find that they do not know, and cannot articulate, their competitive advantage! How can a company or salesperson expect prospects and customers to give their time and attention if they do not understand, clearly and concisely, what that company can do for them that no one else can do? So, how can you demonstrate your competitive advantage? Buy *Sales Differentiation* by Lee Salz, read it page by page, implement its 19 strategies, and you will then be able to set yourself apart from your competition and clearly show your customers what your company can do for them that no one else can do."

—**DR. TONY ALESSANDRA**, author of *Collaborative Selling: How to Gain the Competitive Advantage in Sales*

"Lee Salz has written a different sales book about how YOU can be a different sales professional to help you sell more. It's a common trap that a lot of salespeople fall into, all saying the same things, trying the same strategies and selling in the same way. The problem is that doesn't often work and it's usually those who do it differently that win. This book is brilliantly written and talks you through how you make WHAT you sell different and the WAY you sell different to win more deals. I've read a lot of sales books over the years, but none have given such a great process that I know I'll be able to use straight away."

—**DANIEL DISNEY**, founder of The Daily Sales and leading social selling trainer

"In a sales world with so much noise, Lee's book stands out just like his teachings. It's actionable and easy to read, made for any level of sales professional."

—**MAX ALTSCHULER**, CEO of Sales Hacker and author of *Hacking Sales*

"*Sales Differentiation* is full of ideas that will immediately help you win more business. For example, Lee's Sales Crime Theory—do your investigating before you make the sales call—is so simple and effective, yet a large majority of sales executives think that doing one's homework is finding a phone number or, at best, visiting a prospect's website. Lee gives you easy-to-implement ideas that will ensure you are relevant, that give you permission to ask challenging questions, that give you an edge in negotiations, and that separate you from just about every salesperson in every sales call, every time."

—**SAM RICHTER**, CEO SBR Worldwide/Know More and world's leading expert on sales intelligence

SALES DIFFERENTIATION

SALES

DIFFERENTIATION

19 POWERFUL STRATEGIES
TO WIN MORE DEALS
AT THE PRICES YOU WANT

LEE B. SALZ

HarperCollins
Leadership
An Imprint of HarperCollins

Published by HarperCollins Leadership, an imprint of HarperCollins.

Book design by Elyse J. Strongin, Neuwirth & Associates.

ISBN 978-0-8144-3991-3 (eBook)

Library of Congress Control Number: 2018942034

ISBN 978-0-8144-3990-6

Printed in the United States of America
18 19 20 21 22 LSC 10 9 8 7 6 5 4 3 2 1

TO MY CHILDREN, JAMIE, STEVEN, AND DAVID

*You inspire me every day to be the best I can be in every aspect of life.
I hope I do the same for you. Follow your heart and,
whatever you do, give it everything you have.*

TO MY WIFE, SHARON

*Thank you for supporting all my life ventures and being my life partner.
If you can dream it, you can have it!*

TO MY PARENTS, JOSEPH AND MYRA SALZ

*It means the world to me knowing that you are always behind me.
Thank you!*

TO MY SISTER, MARLO SALZ

I couldn't have asked for a better sister. You're awesome!

TO MY IN-LAWS, PAUL AND GAIL PERSHES

You inspire me to push myself to be better today than I was yesterday.

ACKNOWLEDGMENTS

Many people contributed to *Sales Differentiation* and I'm forever grateful for their involvement in this book venture:

Dawn Deeter-Schmelz, J.J. Vanier distinguished professor and director, National Strategic Selling Institute, Kansas State University

Mike Moroz, CEO, Walters Recycling and Refuse, Inc.

Dave Kirsch, CEO, Shippers Supply, Inc.

Myra Salz, my mom and editor extraordinaire

My sincere thanks to all my clients and their salespeople who have embraced my sales differentiation philosophy and are winning more deals at the prices they want.

Thank you to Jill Konrath who took my call over ten years ago and shared pearls of wisdom that I continue to treasure today.

Thank you to Jeb Blount for contributing an outstanding foreword for *Sales Differentiation*.

CONTENTS

FOREWORD

"You guys are all the same." I'd heard the words come out of the mouths of my prospects more times than I wanted to admit. This was usually followed by, "I really just need your best prices."

I was twenty-five years old and still getting my legs under me as a sales professional. Like most sales reps, what I sold wasn't special or sexy. It was a service that most businesses used, but virtually all considered a commodity that was low on the priority list.

The competition was fierce and aggressive. Every deal was a dogfight. Making things worse was the fact that the sales collateral and pitch for each of the players in the market, including my company, were essentially the same. It was no wonder that buyers perceived no real difference between us.

I learned quickly that the only way to make it was to play the numbers game. You had to touch as many prospects as possible. The problem was that with so many aggressive competitors calling on prospects, getting through and scoring an appointment was almost impossible. I had to make hundreds of prospecting calls, endure endless voicemails, and get through a gauntlet of rude gatekeepers, just for a handful of appointments, only to be told, "You guys are all the same, I need your lowest price."

I'll admit that even though I worked for a well-known brand, had a protected territory, liked my boss, and the commissions were good, I was frustrated and ready to quit. It was a grind that felt more like throwing stuff against the wall and hoping something would stick, than selling.

I was at the end of my rope when one of the senior account executives on our team, Rick, took me under his wing and changed the way I looked at sales. He taught me the art of differentiating by engaging my prospects with more impactful questions about their business challenges. I learned how to slow down the process and engage in meaningful conversations that created value for my customer.

Rick taught me to stop selling my service—which was perceived as a commodity—and start tailoring differentiated solutions focused on the problems and challenges I'd uncovered during conversations with my buyers. Suddenly I looked different. My presentations and messages painted over the pattern of sameness and changed perceptions. I became an expert who solved business problems rather than just another sales rep pushing a tired old commodity.

The following year I was named Account Executive of the Year and set my company's all-time record for new sales. I never looked back.

I have no doubt that you've experienced the same frustration after being told that you and your competitors all look the same. You've experienced how degrading it feels to have your entire value as a sales professional come down to price. This all stops with *Sales Differentiation*. In this book, Lee Salz becomes your mentor (as Rick was to me) and helps you analyze every phase of your interaction with buyers. You'll learn the keys to delivering value that gets you noticed, how to find differentiators within your business, and strategies to position them in a compelling way.

Through nineteen powerful concepts, Lee shows you how every phase of the sales process presents the opportunity to create true differentiation. From the first phone call to a prospect, to an RFP response, to the request for references, there are opportunities to be different from the competition . . . and those differences become the reasons to buy from you.

Lee challenges you to internalize a simple yet profound lesson: *People don't know how to buy what you sell. It's your job to help people buy.*

Buyers need an expert to guide their decision-making. You must provoke and help them gain awareness of the pain and frustration they feel, challenges that are holding them back, and opportunities they are missing. You must position yourself as a problem solver. This earns you a seat at the table from which you shape buyer decision criteria. And this is how you separate yourself from the competition and never look the same again.

I've known Lee and followed his work for more than ten years. He has a tremendous ability to make complex concepts simple and break them into a system that is easy to actualize with real buyers in the real world. In this book, Lee doesn't disappoint. He weaves the lessons together with engaging stories that reach out and pull you in, making this a book you will find very difficult to put down.

—Jeb Blount,
CEO of Sales Gravy and author of *Fanatical Prospecting*

I.

WHAT
YOU SELL

CHAPTER 1

THE BEST SALES CONSULTANT
IN THE WORLD

I appreciate you buying my book to help you refine your selling strategy. If you are like most people who buy a sales book, you are probably asking yourself what makes this author different from all the other sales consultants out there. After all, there are thousands of us. I can easily answer that question for you as I get asked it frequently. Simply put . . .

I'm the best sales consultant in the world!

You read that right. I'm the best sales consultant in the world.

Love Me or Hate Me

As you read my differentiation statement, how do you feel about me? Are you excited to continue reading this book or have I just turned you off? If there was a video camera on you, I bet I would have seen you make the same face a child makes when eating Brussels sprouts for the first time. Eww!

If I asked you to describe me based on my differentiation statement, would you describe me positively with expressions like knowledgeable, helpful, and expert? Or would you use words like cocky, arrogant, and pompous? Most people would select the latter.

Yet, don't you make the same misstep with your buyers? How do you think your buyers feel about you when you come marching into their offices preaching that your company and products are the best? Guess what? They feel the same way about you that you felt about me when I said I was the best.

When I introduced myself to you as the best sales consultant in the world, rather than endearing myself to you and exciting you to want to learn from me, I irritated you. I turned your eagerness to dive in and read my book into skepticism. You may have even wanted to return the book and get a refund. Given how you feel, consider how difficult your selling job becomes when you've annoyed your buyer.

> When salespeople say "best," they think they are building relationships and endearing themselves to their buyers, but their engagement strategy backfires.

When I present this "best" exercise to audiences, it's a fascinating experience. As I'm welcomed to the stage, I see smiles throughout the audience and excitement fills the room. When I take them through this "best" story, the smiles immediately turn to shock. "Did he really just say that he is the best sales consultant in the world?" The smiles return to their faces and they become intrigued as I related my use of "best" to their use of it with buyers. From the stage, the audience dynamic, from excitement to frustration back to excitement, is cool to watch because, like you, they get it now.

Turning Buyers Off

During my programs, when I ask salespeople to share their goals for a first buyer meeting, they say that they want to be different from all the other salespeople calling on the buyer. Yet, right in the first few minutes of the meeting, they say their company and products are the best, making them sound like every other salesperson.

In the history of business, no salesperson has ever said to a prospective buyer, "Our service is pretty good. Our technology is so-so. Our quality is ok. How many would you like to buy?" All salespeople describe what they sell as the best of the best of the best.

When salespeople say "best," they think they are building relationships and endearing themselves to their buyers, but their engagement strategy backfires—sometimes without them even knowing it. Instead of attracting buyers, they unintentionally repel them.

Why can't we say "best?" Because we can't prove it! I can't prove to you that I'm the best sales consultant in the world. Unless an independent study was conducted that analyzed every aspect of your product, your company, and your industry, you can't make a believable representation that *WHAT you sell* is the best. You may be able to say the word "best," but your buyers aren't buying it. What they are really thinking when you say "best" is, "Of course, she says her product is the best. She wants me to buy it, so she gets a commission check."

I once asked the CEO of a technology staffing company why buyers select his firm for development projects. He smiled. "Our people," he said. "We have the best people." He noticed that I had a look of disbelief on my face in response. I asked how he could prove that his people are the best. The CEO was perplexed.

"Do you think your competitors' salespeople say their people are the worst?" I asked further. At that moment, he realized his strategy to stand out in a very competitive market needed work. To win deals at the prices he wanted, he needed to flesh out a strategy such that buyers would perceive meaningful value.

Don't misunderstand my point about the word "best." Salespeople should be passionate about the companies they sell for and the products they represent. If, in your heart, you don't believe *WHAT you sell* is the best, you may be selling for the wrong company. However, being passionate about your company is not the same as making claims with no proof. This is one of the big reasons why the sales profession struggles to earn trust with buyers. The long history of salespeople making unfounded claims has led buyers to be skeptical.

Think about times when you've been on the buying side of the table and heard a salesperson describe her product as "best." Did you "buy" it? I'm guessing you didn't. My bet is you rolled your eyes and thought, "Here we go." You may have even challenged the salesperson on her "best" representation . . . while you do the same thing with your buyers.

The One Person Who Can Say "Best"

I've spent an extended amount of time researching the "best" issue. Over several years, I searched the entire planet and found the one person in the world who can say "best" and buyers listen to the word as gospel. That person is someone you know. Actually, you know that person very well: That person is your client.

When clients describe your company and its products as "the best," buyers pay attention because it's believable. That's why you get referrals. That's also why buyers invest the time to talk with your references.

Consider this: You and your client both say your product is the best. When you say it to a buyer, it's meaningless. It's met with skepticism. When your client says it about you, it's meaningful and gives a buyer confidence in buying from you.

Stranger Influences

We've all bought from Amazon. Every item on the Amazon website has a glowing product description from the manufacturer. Yet, almost none of us put the product in our virtual shopping cart based on the product description. Before we buy, we read purchaser reviews. Reviews from complete strangers influence our decision of whether or not to buy.

My teenage sons play high school baseball. Every fall, they search online for their next bat for the upcoming season. Every bat, as described by the manufacturer, is the most durable, has the most "pop," and feels the lightest in your hands. Even at their young ages, they read the manufacturers' descriptions with a jaded eye. They read the reviews and those reviews affect their bat purchase decision. Great reviews lead them to say, "Dad, this is the best one!"

If you doubt that positioning "best" is a flawed sales strategy, try it with a procurement agent—a professional buyer—and watch the reaction. My prediction is that you will notice an eye roll, followed by a deep sigh of frustration, and a glance at her watch, setting this up to be a very short meeting.

Being Different

Given the goal of being different than all the other salespeople calling on this buyer, let's do just that. Be different! Don't refer to your product as "best" or say that it is better than the competition. Position "different" with your buyers in a meaningful way so they arrive at the conclusion that your solution is the best without you saying the word. For example . . .

> "I'm not going to tell you that our product is the best because I'm sure every other salesperson tells you that. Today, I will share with you some differences in what we offer that our clients find beneficial, and you can decide for yourself if those are meaningful to you."

That perspective sets the tone for a constructive, different meeting, so share it early in the conversation. This approach completely disarms buyers. They find it refreshing! It communicates, "Let's put down our swords and see if there is potential for us to do business together." It helps your buyer laser-in on the differences rather than having to mine for them.

Which differentiators should you mention? How do you position them in a meaningful, compelling fashion? There are countless ways to differentiate yourself from the competition. Positioning meaningful value of the differentiators you have in *WHAT you sell* is exactly what you'll learn in the next several chapters. The differentiators could be in the product or service you sell. They could be in the expertise your company possesses. They can even be found in the way you structure a contract.

The rest of this book teaches you how to put together your sales differentiation strategy so that you have the tools to effectively position *different* to win more deals at the prices you want. After reading this book, you may even say that Lee Salz is the best sales consultant in the world. Of course, that is much more meaningful than if I say it.

Each chapter concludes with the presentation of one of nineteen sales differentiation concepts that comprise this sales philosophy. These concepts serve as the backbone in the development of your sales differentiation strategy.

SALES DIFFERENTIATION CONCEPT #1

Position meaningful differentiation so buyers perceive your solution is "best"—without you saying the word.

CHAPTER 2

DIFFERENTIATION IS MARKETING'S RESPONSIBILITY, ISN'T IT?

When I first met the CEO of a large technology services company, I asked her who was responsible for differentiation in her company. She quickly said, "That's the job of the marketing department."

"You're partially right," I responded, "but what about the sales department?"

A puzzled look appeared on her face. She had not considered "sales" with respect to differentiation strategy.

The conversation with that CEO was not unique. Most executives think the sole responsibility for differentiation resides with marketing. They don't realize that there is a second accountable party for differentiation: the people in sales. When I share that there is a sales component to differentiation, most executives quickly agree with me because they think that marketing creates the differentiation strategy for salespeople to execute. However, they are missing a critical opportunity to help their salespeople win more deals at the prices they want.

Marketing develops and executes a strategy to build brand and name recognition, and to attract the masses with differentiation messaging. It has one-directional communication with prospective buyers through websites, collateral material, and trade shows. Marketing uses its virtual megaphone to amplify the company's differentiation story for all to hear. The thought behind this approach is that it paves the way for salespeople to have meaningful conversations with buyers. However, the differentiation strategy is incomplete. Marketing differentiation intrigues buyers to take a look at what you have to offer, but it does not pop the checkbook open.

Introducing Sales Differentiation

Marketing's role with differentiation is important, but you need another differentiation strategy to win more deals at the prices you want. That strategy is what I call "sales differentiation." It's an extension of the one that marketing develops. Unfortunately, however, it is rarely provided to salespeople. Unlike marketing differentiation, sales differentiation has two-directional communication with an individual, prospective buyer. Marketing differentiation intrigues buyers, but sales differentiation gets them to take action.

A sales differentiation strategy has two components. The first addresses *WHAT you sell*—the aspects of the offering. It identifies who would be interested in those aspects and when they would be interested. And it offers strategy on how to position those aspects in a compelling fashion.

The second component deals with *HOW you sell*. It addresses every interaction you have with buyers and provides ways to create a valuable, differentiated experience for them. From the initial contact, to face-to-face meetings, to presenting solutions, and even with a buyer's request for references, there are ways to stand out from the competition.

Within *HOW you sell* sales differentiation strategy, there is an element that is often missed. It's *YOU*, the salesperson. Every salesperson has the potential to provide meaningful value to buyers in a multitude of ways beyond what their company brings to bear.

The components of sales differentiation empower you to personalize the buying experience such that people perceive meaningful value and buy from you at higher price points. Here's an example of marketing differentiation and sales differentiation working hand in glove.

Car Trouble

In the 1990s, luxury car brands like Lexus and Mercedes discovered they had a major problem. They had shifted their business model from selling cars to leasing them. When you sell a car, it doesn't come back to the dealership. When you lease one, it returns two or three years later. And you must sell it or become financially upside-down on the vehicle.

These car companies saw tremendous value in the returned cars, but also faced a major obstacle when trying to sell them at the prices they wanted. These cars were not new, and the marketplace had an established expression to describe them: "used cars." Used cars are often seen as old and damaged . . . a jalopy, if you will. These luxury car companies contended that their returned cars were different and had greater value than a traditional used car. In most cases, the leased cars had low mileage and were in great shape.

To sell these cars at the prices they wanted, they needed to reach a different buyer with a different message. They needed to reach those people who could afford to purchase a new car, not necessarily a new luxury vehicle, but people with a stronger financial situation than those targeted for used cars. To that end, they created the moniker "certified pre-owned" for these cars. The differentiation strategy worked tremendously well. These were still "used cars," but through differentiation messaging, they were perceived by buyers as having more value. This strategy helped car companies sell these cars at the prices they wanted.

Coming back to the difference between marketing and sales differentiation, marketing differentiation intrigued buyers enough to consider a certified pre-owned vehicle. However, it was sales differentiation that led to a particular car being purchased. After all, buyers had numerous choices. They could have selected multiple cars on a Lexus lot or a

Mercedes lot. They also could have purchased a new vehicle elsewhere. It was sales differentiation that led to each car being sold—converting intrigue into action.

Execution of the sales differentiation strategy was the burden placed on each car salesperson. They had to engage buyers in a way that allowed them to position meaningful differentiators. The discussed differentiators were different for each buyer based on who they were and what was important to them.

Sales Differentiation Dissected

As I mentioned earlier, sales differentiation involves two-directional communication with an individual, prospective buyer, while marketing differentiation offers one-directional communication. In two-directional communication, a buyer answers questions; the information she shares helps to provide the salesperson with the necessary tools for a sales differentiation strategy. The context of the questions and the responses to them direct the conversation between buyer and seller rather than "one-size-fits-all" messaging.

How do salespeople know what to ask prospective buyers and how to position differentiators if the company has not documented its strategy? They don't. That's why weak sales pipelines and lowering prices to win deals are rampant issues in most sales organizations.

The second part of the sales differentiation definition references "an individual, prospective buyer" rather than for the masses. This calls for salespeople to position relevant differentiation elements with a specific person rather than spewing the same pitch to everyone.

How do salespeople know which differentiators resonate with which prospective buyers and under what circumstances those matter without having a documented sales differentiation strategy in place? They don't. That results in prospective buyers feeling disconnected from salespeople and not buying from them. Being able to connect with a buyer is a critical factor for salespeople when it comes to winning deals at the prices you want.

In most e-commerce and some retail sales, marketing differentiation and sales differentiation converge because the expectation is that these transactions are conducted without a salesperson's involvement. In business-to-business selling, that is not the expectation. The need for sales differentiation justifies the core function of salespeople.

My Challenge to You

Chances are, you and I have never met. I don't know the company for which you sell or the industry that it is part of. Yet, I know something about your industry that you do not. I know, down to the penny, how much companies have spent in the past year on the products you sell. I make that bold statement with total confidence in my knowledge. You may think you know it, but I'm certain that you don't.

As I said, I know for certain what companies spent on your products. I'm sure you are pausing to think of your number. Allow me to share what companies spent on *WHAT you sell* . . . ZERO! *Companies* don't buy anything. *People* do. That is what makes sales differentiation so important. Sales differentiation engages the people who influence the decision to buy. I refer to these people as "Decision Influencers" (DIs). You will see this expression used throughout the rest of the book synonymously with "buyer."

> The need for sales differentiation justifies the core function of salespeople.

Every DI is different and the strategy to engage each one needs to be different as well given their roles and responsibilities. The key to winning deals at the prices you want resides in your ability to engage every DI in a meaningful way, so they support your solution being adopted.

However, there are several obstacles that impede your ability to do that. Recent studies highlight that point:

- Forrester said that 74 percent of buyers conduct more than half of their research online before talking with a salesperson.
- The Corporate Executive Board (CEB) found that 6.8 people are involved on the buying side in the average B2B decision-making process.
- According to Corporate Visions, 74 percent of buyers chose the first salesperson who adds value and insight.

There's nothing salespeople can do to prevent buyers from researching online, nor can they affect the number of people involved in decision-making. But there is much that salespeople can do to be the first to add value and insight. They do that through sales differentiation.

You can't be too early when differentiating, but you can be too late.

Over the years, sales managers have tried many ways to win more deals at the prices they want. They've screamed at their salespeople to sell the value. The message heard by the salespeople is to beat up the buyers until they see what we see. That approach doesn't work.

Another strategy that won't work: salespeople waiting for price to become an issue and *then* trying to differentiate themselves. You can't be too early when differentiating, but you can be too late. Once buyers have sticker shock, it's nearly impossible for them to become receptive to learning about your differences.

Why Sales Differentiation Matters

After I define sales differentiation in my strategy development programs, I ask executives and salespeople why sales differentiation is important. "To win deals!" they say. Their answer is partially right. Yes, the purpose is to win deals, but there are two parts to that purpose. Sales differentiation is not just about winning deals, but also at the prices you want.

Have you ever been in this situation? You had to fight hard to win the deal, but when you tell your manager the great news, instead of receiving accolades, you get a snarky response. "You won the deal," he says, "but look how low we had to drop our price to win it." It's a horrible feeling for salespeople when the company doesn't love the piece of business they've just brought in. Sales differentiation helps to eliminate the need for those uncomfortable conversations.

> Sales differentiation is not just about winning deals, but also at the prices you want.

One of the true tests of whether or not your sales differentiation strategy is working is if your buyer asks you to match a price from your competitor. Every time you hear that request, you know the strategy failed because the buyer sees no meaningful difference between you and the competition.

Salespeople ask me, "If we are the low-price provider in the marketplace, do we still need a sales differentiation strategy?"

I then ask them, "How many of you are living in the cheapest home, driving the cheapest car, eating the cheapest food, and wearing the cheapest clothes?" Of course, none of them are. Even if you are selling the low-price product, you need a sales differentiation strategy to ensure you win more deals at the prices you want.

In the next chapter, you will learn of the frustration that is plaguing the sales profession and how that affects salespeople's ability to perceive meaningful value in what they sell.

SALES DIFFERENTIATION CONCEPT #2

Sales differentiation converts buyer intrigue into buyer action to win more deals at the prices you want.

CHAPTER 3

THE ROOT CAUSE OF
A SALESPERSON'S FRUSTRATION

Rejection is a way of life in sales. Many days end in frustration: You bust your hump in pursuit of deals and come up empty-handed. While there are many rough days for salespeople, there is one day that stands out as the absolute worst.

What is that day? I love to challenge salespeople with that question. They'll say it's the day they lose a deal they thought they would win, or when they miss quota by a smidge. Some will humorously say the worst day is the day they have a new sales manager.

While all of those (including getting a new manager) can be painful, there is one that is even worse. It's the day a salesperson wakes up and says to himself, "I sell a commodity." In other words, the only thing Decision Influencers care about is price.

It's horrible when salespeople feel that way because, in their minds, buyers see no value in what's being sold to them. If you've ever felt that way or you feel that way now, consider this: What isn't a commodity? Computers, cars, hotels, appliances, furniture, staffing services, cellphones, airlines, janitorial services . . . the list goes on and on. These can all be considered commodities for the sole reason that this is a function of the way our minds work when we buy.

The Difference Between Buying and Selling

Looking at the buy-sell spectrum, when we are on the buyer side of the table, we put together a decision matrix. Some of us do it in our heads while others put pen to paper. In the left-hand column, we list our decision criteria . . . our requirements, if you will. In the column headers, we list all the places where we can buy it.

Within the matrix, we mark the matches between our decision criteria and the places where we can acquire it. Our fundamental goal is to identify the best price based on our decision criteria. When we wear the buyer hat, our enemy is differentiation. We don't want differences; we want sameness! That sameness makes it easy to compare and contrast with a decision made obvious for us. Differentiation translates into options that make the decision process challenging as we try to select the best price for what we want to buy.

When we are on the sales side of the table, our fundamental goal is differentiation. We want to implode the grid by demonstrating meaningful value. We never want to fit within the matrix. Sameness, better stated as "commodity," is our adversary. We want to stand out from the competition and justify our price point. The core difference between the way people buy and sell means that when using sales differentiation techniques, salespeople need to take care not to frustrate buyers. A salesperson's level of care, when using sales differentiation, is critical to success.

Searching for "The One Thing"

Finding meaningful value in *WHAT you sell* can be difficult for salespeople. There is a question they ask themselves in search of it and it is that very question that is the root cause of their frustration. It's the search for "the one thing."

In the Billy Crystal classic *City Slickers*, several men set off into the wilderness in search for the one thing that will give their life meaning.

Salespeople, in their quest to develop an effective sales strategy, are also searching for that one thing that will give their sale meaningful value. While in the movie the men find their answer, the salespeople are not so lucky—and there is a very good reason why.

This search for "one thing" makes salespeople miserable because it is based on a flawed question. Salespeople ask themselves, "What makes us unique?" Unique is a tall order. Look up the word in Webster's dictionary and you find definitions like "existing as the only one," "having no like or equal," and "incomparable." Given those definitions, who among us is selling something that meets those criteria? It's very, very few of us. No wonder salespeople are so frustrated. They are searching for something that, for most of us, doesn't exist.

If you are lucky enough to be selling something that is patented, by definition you have something that is unique. However, patents expire after a period of time. That's how generic drugs come to market. Plus, just because you have a patent doesn't mean *WHAT you sell* provides meaningful value to buyers.

The "unique question" is one that salespeople ask their management teams as well as themselves. They hope that, in response to their queries, they will be given magical words to say to Decision Influencers that will lead salespeople to hitting quotas with ease and raking in commission dollars. They dream of walking into a DI's office, sharing these magical words, and a checkbook flying open. Unfortunately, that isn't likely to happen. If sales were that easy, companies wouldn't offer salespeople the compensation levels that they do.

When salespeople can't find that "one thing," they get angry, frustrated, and downtrodden. Some even brush off their resumes and begin searching for their next job. They don't realize the flaw is not with the answer they were given, but rather with the question they asked.

As an executive team member, I helped sell a company to a large competitor. Post-acquisition, I was standing in my new employer's conference room with their executive team. "Now that we're all family, I have a question for you. What makes us unique?" I asked. More than twenty years later, I'm still waiting for an answer. It wasn't their fault for not having a response; it was mine. I asked the wrong question. What I should have asked is, "What makes us different?"

Unique versus Different

Perhaps you've just rolled your eyes. You're thinking that "unique" and "different" mean the same thing and that I'm splitting hairs. I challenge you to look those up on Thesaurus.com. On that website, a search of the word "different" (there isn't an entry for "differentiator") does not return a synonym of "unique," but you do find the word "contrasting."

The word "unique" means you are the only one in the world to possess a certain quality or aspect. The word "different" is used to denote a comparison to something like a buyer's current solution or the incumbent provider. The good news is that uniqueness is not a requirement for an effective sales differentiation strategy. Uniqueness is not needed at all to win more deals at the prices you want.

The "Unique versus Different" table (Figure 3-1) highlights this distinction. It compares and contrasts five people along six decision criteria.

FIGURE 3-1: **Unique versus Different**

	JOHN	HARRY	PHIL	MARY	STEVE
EYES	2	2	2	2	2
HAIR	Brown	Brown	Brown	Black	Brown
GENDER	Male	Male	Male	Female	Male
RESIDES	NY	GA	NY	GA	MA
HEIGHT	5'8"	5'9"	6'0"	5'9"	5'8"
HOBBY	Baseball	Hockey	Golf	Golf	Hockey

Reviewing the data, you see all five of them have two eyes. All of them have brown hair except Mary. Four of them are men and one is a woman. Two of them live in New York and two reside in Georgia, while one lives in Massachusetts. Two of them are five-foot eight inches tall and two are five-foot nine inches tall, with one of them a six-footer. Two enjoy hockey and golf, while one is a baseball aficionado.

There are five attributes that meet the definition of unique: black hair, female, Massachusetts, six-footer, and baseball. Only Mary possesses more than one of those unique attributes (see Figure 3-2).

FIGURE 3-2: **Unique versus Different—Unique Attributes**

	JOHN	HARRY	PHIL	MARY	STEVE
EYES	2	2	2	2	2
HAIR	Brown	Brown	Brown	Black	Brown
GENDER	Male	Male	Male	Female	Male
RESIDES	NY	GA	NY	GA	MA
HEIGHT	5'8"	5'9"	6'0"	5'9"	5'8"
HOBBY	Baseball	Hockey	Golf	Golf	Hockey

Taking a closer look at the data, Harry possesses no unique attributes. Every attribute in Harry's column can also be found in someone else's. Does that mean Harry isn't special? Does that mean he provides no meaningful value?

Analyzing the data another way, look at all the attributes in Harry's column (see Figure 3-3). Other than Harry, which person can say they have two eyes, brown hair, are a man, live in Georgia, are five-foot nine inches tall, and enjoy hockey? None of them can! The aggregate of the data presents Harry's differentiated story. It's his meaningful value.

FIGURE 3-3: Unique versus Different—Harry's Differentiated Value

	JOHN	HARRY	PHIL	MARY	STEVE
EYES	2	2	2	2	2
HAIR	Brown	Brown	Brown	Black	Brown
GENDER	Male	Male	Male	Female	Male
RESIDES	NY	GA	NY	GA	MA
HEIGHT	5'8"	5'9"	6'0"	5'9"	5'8"
HOBBY	Baseball	Hockey	Golf	Golf	Hockey

As a matter of fact, each of those five people can position a differentiated story based on the aggregate of the data (see Figure 3-4). They each have a differentiated story to share that no one else can tell the same way.

FIGURE 3-4: Unique versus Different—The Differentiated Story

	JOHN	HARRY	PHIL	MARY	STEVE
EYES	2	2	2	2	2
HAIR	Brown	Brown	Brown	Black	Brown
GENDER	Male	Male	Male	Female	Male
RESIDES	NY	GA	NY	GA	MA
HEIGHT	5'8"	5'9"	6'0"	5'9"	5'8"
HOBBY	Baseball	Hockey	Golf	Golf	Hockey

Putting This Into Practice

The "Unique versus Different" matrix is a metaphor for the question salespeople should be seeking to answer. Search for the aggregate story you can position with Decision Influencers, in a compelling fashion, that no one else can tell in the same way. Instead of searching for the one unique aspect that isn't likely to be found, look for the aggregate, differentiated story you can position. Later in the book, I teach you how to position your differentiated story in a meaningful way with DIs. After all, it's one thing to have a compelling differentiation story, but it's another to help a DI see the compelling value in it as well.

> Instead of searching for the one unique aspect that isn't likely to be found, look for the aggregate, differentiated story to be positioned.

To implement this approach into your selling system, develop a matrix similar to the "Unique versus Different" matrix. In the left-hand column, list the important buyer decision criteria. In the top row, list yourself and your competitors. Mark the boxes that match for each decision criterion relative to the competition and yourself. As you go through this analysis, the hope is that, based on the aggregate, you find that you have a differentiated story that your competitors cannot tell in the same way.

For those who cannot develop their differentiated story, there is Plan B: Simply drop your price. No one is going to pay more for something perceived as identical to something else. If you don't want to drop your price under those conditions, work on your business to create a compelling, differentiated story. Or shut your doors. There is no other choice. The good news is that I have yet to find a company that doesn't have an opportunity to develop a compelling sales differentiation strategy factoring both *WHAT you sell* and *HOW you sell.*

Of course, salespeople are hyper-concerned about price points for what they sell. In the next chapter, you will learn that when it comes to buyer decision-making, price isn't as important as you may think.

SALES DIFFERENTIATION CONCEPT #3

Sales differentiation is not about being unique, but rather being different, relative to other buyer options.

CHAPTER 4

WHAT WOULD YOU PAY FOR SOMETHING YOU COULD GET FOR FREE?

The sales differentiation philosophy presented in this book, thus far, has been focused around price and value strategies. Let's go to the other extreme.

What would you be willing to pay for something you could have for free?

I challenge salespeople and executives with this question and they bristle in their response. "I wouldn't pay anything for something I could get for free." I then ask them to rethink their answer because I am certain that they do. They look puzzled after being challenged again. I then place a bottle of water in front of them. That's when the light bulbs go on.

Drinkable water is readily available in kitchens across the United States. Yet, according to *Beverage Marketing Corp*, over $12.8 billion was spent on bottled water in the United States in 2016 making it the largest beverage category by volume. Despite the easy access we have to free water, the U.S. was the largest purchaser of bottled water in the world according to *Business Insider*.

Some of you may argue that you pay for the water in your home, which is true. Having checked the water bill for my home, the price is $1.20 for a thousand gallons. That's less than a penny per gallon. You may pay a little more or less, but for all intents and purposes, the water you drink out of your faucet is free.

More Expensive Than Gasoline

"If we take into account the fact that almost two thirds of all bottled water sales are single 16.9-ounce (500 mL) bottles, though, this cost is much, much higher: about $7.50 per gallon," according to the American Water Works Association. "That's almost twice the cost of a gallon of regular gasoline."

ConvergEx Group Chief Market Strategist Nick Colas said, "What's most remarkable about this data, though, is what it says about the American consumer: that despite the (debatably) excessively high cost of bottled water when compared to its tap equivalent, we continue to buy it—even during an economic downturn."

Watered Down

Furthering Colas's point, most people who buy bottled water don't even know the source of it. For all we know, someone has broken into our homes, attached hoses to our kitchen faucets, filled the bottles with water, and sold the water back to us. I used to share that anecdote with audiences in jest. Then, I came across this:

In 2007, ABC News reported that Aquafina was now required to change its labeling to reflect the fact that its bottled water comes from a public water source.

Dasani soon followed suit as their water comes from local water sources as well. In other words, what I said in jest was theoretically true. While no one had actually broken into our homes to steal our water, we were being sold water we already had in our kitchens. We are not only paying for something we could have had for free. We already possessed it and bought it anyway.

The Many Ways We Buy Free Water

Water is commonly purchased by the case at supermarkets. A case of twenty-four bottles costs about five dollars. Amortizing the cost of the case of water, the price per bottle is twenty cents each. Again, this is for water we already have for free.

I began by asking you what you would pay for something you could get for free, to which you thought to yourself that you wouldn't pay anything. I shared data with you showing that we spend a fortune on something we could get for free. Not only are we willing to pay for something we could have for free, we are willing to spend ten times the price to get it. Yes, we are!

Visit any gas station. You will find the same bottle of water that was twenty cents when bought by the case, sold for ten times the price. If you don't believe people buy bottled water at gas stations, I challenge you to find a gas station (or convenience store) that does not sell bottled water. They all do because we buy our water there, too.

We've also come up with another way to spend money on something we could have had for free: refillable water bottles. These come in all shapes and sizes, and in every color under the rainbow. A well-made refillable water bottle costs about twenty dollars. Contrasting the refillable bottle to a prefilled bottle of water, from a return on investment perspective, we could have a hundred prefilled bottles of water (bought by the case at the supermarket for twenty cents each) for the price of one refillable bottle of water. Again, all of this cost is for water we already have for free.

Why We Buy It

Why do we buy this product? One reason is portion management. It's not practical to cup our hands and hold our water as we walk around the office. It would splash and leak. Not to mention, it would be impossible to get any work done. Water contained in a bottle has a lid or cap on it. This makes it easy to be mobile with the water and prevent spills.

The bottles also come in different sizes, so we can buy the portion we desire. This is especially important for those with young children who have a habit of taking two sips from a full-sized bottle of water and throwing away the rest. Smaller bottles help us minimize our waste (and their spills).

Another reason people buy this product is convenience. You're driving down the road feeling parched. You don't want to make a production out of quenching your thirst. You want to get something to drink quickly and a short stop at the gas station's convenience store will do the trick.

Some people say that the taste of bottled water drives their decision to buy it. In other words, some people think that bottled water tastes better than water from the tap. Yet, some of the major brands for this water are selling us tap water. Having grown up in New York City and New Jersey, I can attest that people from that part of the country say that

People are willing to spend more money for what they perceive to be meaningful value.

nothing tastes better than their tap water, but they buy bottled water just like everyone else for the reasons already mentioned.

When it comes to refillable bottles, sometimes ecology drives the decision to buy them. There has been a lot of press about discarded water bottles filling landfills and polluting our waterways at alarming rates. Some people also like that they can get refillable bottles to match their favorite color or shape.

Price Matters . . . or Does It?

What does this water story tell us relative to sales differentiation? Salespeople are often sensitive about the subject of price. Being truly honest, they are hypersensitive about it. Even though they say they believe in value, they quickly forget that at the first sign of buyer resistance. If I had a penny for every time a salesperson ran to a manager saying, "We're going to lose this deal if we don't drop our price," I'd be the richest man in the world!

Look at any parking lot. What do you notice about the cars parked in it? No two of them are exactly alike. At their core, each car has a seat, steering wheel, gas pedal, brakes, roof, and doors. Any car you buy is guaranteed to come with those things included in it.

Yet, most people spend more than the minimum required to own the car they want. They make buying decisions for a wide array of reasons beyond the core (just like the bottled water). Some people want a specific color, size, or seat material. Others want a particular sound quality from the stereo system or high-tech safety features. People are willing to spend more money for what they perceive to be meaningful value.

You could make the same case with clothes. Walk the mall. Every person is wearing different clothes. We each could have bought the bare minimum basics, but we don't. Each person has a look or style they strive to have their clothes reinforce. Again, people are willing to spend more money for it.

Milking Profits

Sales differentiation tells us that it's not the price but the perceived meaningful value that drives purchasing decisions. A great example of this is milk. I was shopping at the supermarket and milk was on my grocery list. I opened the refrigerator door and found two skim milk options— name-brand and generic store-brand. I was astonished by the price difference between the two for a gallon of skim milk. The name-brand was priced at $3.69, and the generic was $2.19 for the same quantity. That's $1.50 more for the name-brand, which is a 68 percent price difference. Given my work with sales differentiation, I was intrigued and searched for "the why." There had to be a justification for this astonishing price difference.

Did the name-brand claim to be better tasting? No.

Did it claim to have better cows? No.

According to large print on the name-brand's label, a serving of their milk contained nine grams of protein. The generic didn't promote that "differentiator," but when I looked closely at the generic's ingredients, I found out it also had nine grams of protein per serving. Same!

I studied the two brands from every angle in search of differentiation. Every one of them came up the same, except price. However, the name-brand company had a way to create perceived, meaningful value. They are primarily known for their dairy products, especially ice cream. It appears that their strategy is for buyers to perceive enough value in their milk because of the ice cream experience, that they are willing to pay more for it. Because you love the dairy products that the company produces, and you assume that the milk used in those products comes from the same cows, the strategy is that the perceived value justifies paying 68 percent more for the same product. I challenge you to find a market that doesn't sell both name-brand and generic store-brand milk.

Keep the water and milk stories in mind the next time you think price is the major obstacle to winning deals at the prices you want. Perceived, meaningful differentiation, not price, drives purchase decisions!

SALES DIFFERENTIATION CONCEPT #4

Buyers will pay more for differentiated solutions that they perceive offer meaningful value.

CHAPTER 5

FINDING YOUR DIFFERENTIATORS

I'm sure you are familiar with the age-old "apples to apples" comparison. The purpose of that analysis is to contrast two seemingly like items to decide which one to buy. Given that, let's consider two apples. Both are the same size, weight, type, shape, color, and flavor. However, one of the apples is priced 20 percent higher than the other. Which apple would you buy? Of course, you would buy the cheaper one, given the sameness of the two.

What if the more expensive apple was organic and that attribute was important to you? Which apple would you buy now? You would buy the more expensive, organic apple.

What if the more expensive apple could be purchased down the street and the cheaper apple was five miles away? Which apple would you buy if you didn't have a car? You would buy the more expensive apple given that you don't have transportation to buy the cheaper one.

In each of these cases, buyer behavior was affected without changing the *core* of the product. None of the six attributes were changed. The apples were still the same size, weight, type, shape, color, and flavor; but buyer decision-making was affected.

The Fruitless Search for Differentiation

Many salespeople only look at the core of what they sell in their search for meaningful differentiation and are frustrated when they cannot find it. Take the apple story as an example. There wasn't any meaningful differentiation when analyzing the core, which is why we elected to purchase the cheaper apple. Price will always be the deciding factor when buyers don't perceive meaningful differentiation.

Price will always be the deciding factor when buyers don't perceive meaningful differentiation.

Sometimes you need to step away from the core of *WHAT you sell* to find your differentiated aspects. When the dreaded price issue arises, as the buyer tells a salesperson that his price is higher than the competitor's, the issue isn't price. It's a symptom of the real issue. What the buyer is telling the salesperson is that she doesn't perceive meaningful differences in what the salesperson has presented. When a buyer sees all decision aspects as equal, price becomes the ultimate decision factor. For most salespeople, that factor is the kiss of death for the sale because what he is selling isn't the cheapest option.

Many sales managers think that salespeople who can't overcome the price issue (a point we explore with greater depth in a later chapter) have an inability to close. These managers hire sales trainers who teach closing techniques to assist with the perceived sales skill gap. The reality is that the price issue isn't the problem at all. It's a symptom. The actual issue is that the salesperson has not differentiated what he sells in a way that resonates with the buyer.

As I covered in an earlier chapter, sales differentiation can't occur too early in the interaction between seller and buyer, but it can occur too late. When the price issue rears its ugly head, the salesperson is, in essence, being told that he failed the "apples to apples" test. In other words, the price issue isn't a closing problem, but rather a symptom of an issue earlier in the buying process—a failure to demonstrate meaningful differentiation with the buyer.

The Sales Differentiation Universe

Moving away from the core attributes of *WHAT you sell* can open doors to creative, extremely effective ways to use sales differentiation to win more deals at the prices you want.

Think about your business and your buyers. Much of *WHAT you sell* probably can't be changed. However, if you take a step back from the core, what can you do to differentiate *WHAT you sell* in a way that matters to Decision Influencers? These aspects must be meaningful enough for someone to justify buying from you at the price you want.

In some cases, your differentiators are obvious, but don't stop there. With some analysis and creativity, you can potentially find plenty more when you look at the six components of what I refer to as the Sales Differentiation Universe. The more robust your sales differentiation strategy the easier it is to demonstrate meaningful value and win more deals at the prices you want.

Before I share the Sales Differentiation Universe with you, a few words of caution: First, not all differentiators will matter to everyone. Second, differentiators will need to be positioned with buyers, not just tossed out as trite expressions, so buyers see the value in them. In later chapters, you will learn how to identify which differentiators matter to whom and when, as well as positioning strategies for your differentiators.

When a buyer sees all decision aspects as equal, price becomes the ultimate decision factor. For most salespeople, that factor is the kiss of death for the sale because what he is selling isn't the cheapest option.

Here are the six components of the Sales Differentiation Universe:

THE COMPANY

- **Credentials** — certifications such as ISO, Six Sigma, and Lean, as well as awards and patents.
- **Size** — revenue, employees, clients, etc.
- **Specialty** — a niche focus on a product, vertical market, buyer type, etc.
- **Expertise** — the solutions offered, industry regulations associated with those solutions, challenges that buyers are trying to resolve, etc.
- **Organization structure** — as it relates to the client experience.
- **Financial strength** — revenue growth, number of clients, profitability, etc.
- **Corporate structure** — publicly traded companies and privately held companies can both differentiate based on the value associated with those structures.
- **Footprint** — location of your corporate, regional, or field offices, and the quantity of them.
- **Scope** — whether you're a local, regional, national, or global player.
- **Strategic partners and acquisitions** — broadening your solution capabilities, footprint, and ability to scale through those relationships.
- **Key clients** — blue-chip names in your portfolio provide credibility.
- **Published studies** — demonstrates expertise and furthers your credibility around the subject matter.
- **Client satisfaction** — how you measure client satisfaction, client retention rates, etc.
- **Charity and community involvement** — investing time and money in the community and charities can be meaningful to buyers.

- **Social responsibility**—causes that your company has championed.
- **Research and development investment**—demonstrates that you are continually looking to improve your products and the business to help your clients stay on the cutting edge.
- **Facility security**—how you ensure access to the locations is protected.

THE PEOPLE

- **Expertise**—the employees in various departments of your company.
- **Hiring practices and employee screening**—how you evaluate prospective employees before extending an offer.
- **Employee onboarding and development**—how employees are assimilated into their respective roles when first hired and the training offered to provide growth opportunities.
- **Employee tenure**—lack of turnover gives comfort to clients.
- **Employee satisfaction and recognition**—how this is measured and the actions taken to show employees they are appreciated.
- **Key employees and certifications**—those who have impressive credentials, a specialized expertise that is helpful to clients, or are well known in the industry.
- **Contractor vs. employees**—are those who work for you direct employees or are they contractor relationships? Both have differentiated stories to be positioned.
- **Employees per manager**—low employee to manager ratios demonstrate high management oversight which infers quality work.
- **Staffing levels**—how this is managed, monitored, and changed to support client needs.

THE PRODUCTS

- **Attributes**—size, shape, color, flavor, strength, variety, weight, materials, etc.
- **Quality**—how this is measured and demonstrated.
- **Using client feedback to improve product**—how you solicit perspectives from clients and use those to improve *WHAT you sell*.
- **Levels or tiers**—low-end versus high-end options with opportunities to support buyers at various spend levels.
- **One-stop shop**—providing a comprehensive solution that reduces the number of providers a buyer needs to work with.
- **Exclusivity**—selling to only one buyer within a geographic area, vertical market, etc., or that only your company can sell a particular offering within a market.
- **Bundling**—ways to construct a product to provide additional value.
- **Customization and configuration**—changing *WHAT you sell* to align with buyer needs.
- **Manufactured location**—where *WHAT you sell* is assembled.
- **Packaging**—the way in which a product is packaged to eliminate breakage or increase appeal.

SERVICE

- **Flexibility**—providing service in the way a buyer wants to receive it.
- **Account management**—proactive involvement with clients.
- **Customer service**—responsive involvement with clients. This includes direct access to representatives, average phone wait times, languages supported, and how representatives can be accessed (phone, online chat, website, etc.).
- **Service days and times**—when service is available to clients.

- **Client onboarding**—the process used to migrate an account from their current provider to your company.
- **Using client feedback to improve service**—how you solicit perspectives from clients and use that information to improve service.
- **Performance metrics**—the system used by the company to measure and monitor performance.
- **Inventory**—amount of *WHAT you sell* that is available immediately.
- **Delivery**—the way *WHAT you sell* can be received and turn-around time for delivery.
- **Reports and analytics**—data that allows the buyer to measure your and their performance.
- **Process efficiency**—steps you've taken so that service is provided cost-effectively and quickly to clients.
- **Safety**—steps taken to provide a safe workplace and how safety is tracked.

TECHNOLOGY

- **Integrations**—technology systems that your system can directly communicate with.
- **Online ordering**—ways buyers can order from you on their own.
- **Languages**—languages supported by your website.
- **Employee developers versus outsourced staff**—there are differentiation opportunities to position with both types.
- **Data storage**—where this is located, how data is backed up, and the frequency of backing up the data.
- **Security**—access to the website, data encryption, and ways you protect private data.
- **Website up-time**—commitment for your website to be available to users.

- **User experience** — ease of use for your clients to navigate the website.
- **Software development process and testing** — the way in which new software is created and deployed to clients.
- **Flexibility** — how the technology can adjust to match the needs of clients.
- **Performance visibility** — how much access clients have to data for their account online.
- **Planned enhancements** — new technology features planned and currently in development.
- **Help desk** — support for users of the website.
- **User guides and tutorials** — offline support for the technology offered.
- **Using client feedback to improve technology** — how you solicit perspectives from clients and use those to improve technology.
- **Mobile** — technology access on phones and tablets.

CONTRACT

- **No contract** — nothing for buyers to sign that commits them to a relationship.
- **Flexible terms** — willing to negotiate contract provisions.
- **Pricing structure** — spend incentives, pricing tiers, rebates, etc.
- **Guarantees and warranties** — your commitments to the quality of *WHAT you sell* and the service that supports it.
- **Service-level provisions** — your commitment to performance of *WHAT you sell* and the service that supports it.
- **Duration** — the initial term of the agreement and the handling of renewal terms.

- **Payment terms**—when payment is due and how it is to be paid.
- **Value ads**—other benefits to be provided in addition to what is being purchased.
- **Cancellation**—conditions for termination.

Three Ways to Build Your List of Differentiators

You probably read through the six components of the Sales Differentiation Universe quickly. I challenge you to go back and read through this section again. Use a highlighter to mark your differentiators in the book. Remember, as you go through this exercise, that you are not searching for *unique*, but rather *different* relative to a buyer's options.

I'm guessing you, just like my sales differentiation workshop clients, can add at least ten differentiators to your list that you are not positioning with buyers today. Of course, not all components of the Universe are applicable to all businesses, but I bet you can find a minimum of ten differentiators that you aren't using today.

A second exercise you can conduct to develop your list of differentiators is a competitor analysis. Select your ten biggest competitors for the exercise. For each one, ask yourself two questions:

1. *Why do you win?*
2. *Why do they win?*

After all, nothing matters other than the outcome. The answers to "why you win" highlight differentiators to add to your list as you've identified those as reasons DIs buy from you.

A third exercise you can perform to identify even more differentiators is an analysis of your DIs. Make a list of everyone who can influence the decision for *WHAT you sell*. Be all-inclusive with your list. Include titles, not just departments. For example, if the marketing department can influence the decision, you may include the department head as well as the marketing analyst on your list of DIs.

As with the prior exercise, ask yourself two questions. First:

As this person lies in bed at night thinking about her role and responsibilities, what is keeping her awake?

This question has nothing to do with you or *WHAT you sell*. It is entirely about the individual DI's concerns and objectives. The answers to this question would be the same regardless of *WHAT you sell*.

The second question is the synergy between the DI's concerns and the solutions you offer.

Given what your company offers, how can you help this DI address her concerns and objectives?

The answers to the synergy question provide even more differentiators for your list.

Earlier, I asked you to construct a matrix that listed buyer decision criteria in the left-hand column. Go back to that exercise and add these new differentiators to the criteria list to strengthen your aggregate story.

The three exercises identify sales differentiation opportunities beyond the basics you may have considered thus far. Without those differentiated aspects, you leave buyers with one primary factor when making a decision: price. And that won't help you win more deals at the prices you want.

SALES DIFFERENTIATION CONCEPT #5

Price is the ultimate decision factor in the absence of differentiation.

CHAPTER 6

WHO CARES ABOUT YOUR DIFFERENTIATORS?

On March 22, 2002, I came across an article in the *Wall Street Journal* that many readers probably passed over. The article announced United Airlines' change in beverage provider from Coke to Pepsi for its airline passengers. This change ended a multi-decade relationship with Coke. The article subject was fascinating to me given world events at that time, so I read it.

Think back to what was happening in the United States in that period. It was approximately six months after 9/11. The airline industry was in a frenzy. Revenues were down due to people not flying because of their fear of terrorism. New regulations were being imposed upon airlines, and their operating costs were soaring through the roof. Yet, someone was able to close a soda deal during this time. This beverage deal is a great story!

Pepsi was running its "Pepsi Challenge" marketing campaign, which was a taste test comparing Pepsi to Coke. As part of the Challenge, people were given a blind taste test, sampling both Pepsi and Coke. The Challenge participants didn't know which cola was which while they drank them. During the Pepsi commercials, the two sodas were revealed after the sampling and viewers saw that Pepsi was the taster's preferred beverage.

Given the success of the Pepsi Challenge campaign, a Pepsi salesperson contacted the CEO of United Airlines. He offered to administer the Challenge for United's executive team. "I'll come to your office with a six-pack of Pepsi and a six-pack of Coke," he said.

"We'll blindfold your team and have them taste each cola. If they prefer Pepsi, you'll agree to switch to Pepsi and serve it to your airline passengers."

The CEO agreed to the Challenge. His team preferred the taste of Pepsi to Coke—and the airline made the beverage change.

If you doubt the credence of that sales story, you're right to do so. Of course, no Pepsi salesperson offered the Challenge to the CEO of United Airlines. Actually, that deal was the result of a joint marketing venture between the two companies intended to drive revenue for both. Driving revenue was a priority for United Airlines at the time. That is what led to the deal.

The Elevator Story Flaw

While the deal strategy I shared is fictitious, it highlights a common sales misstep. Oftentimes, salespeople don't think enough about the person to whom they are positioning their sales differentiation strategy. They have one speech, commonly called an "elevator story" (or pitch), which is shared with all Decision Influencers regardless of whether or not its content is relevant to the listener.

No salesperson should ever have *an* elevator story. That statement probably raised your eyebrow. After all, an elevator story is an accepted sales best practice. The problem isn't the "elevator story" concept, but its singular nature ("an elevator story"). The Pepsi Challenge was effective with consumers because they are the ones purchasing the beverage. But the strategy had no relevancy with airline executives because they aren't selling the product to travelers. Since the executives were not receiving complaints from passengers about the free beverage—no customers threatened to switch airlines over United's soft drinks—they could not have cared less about a taste test.

Before sharing "what you do" with a DI, take a moment to think about the person with whom you are about to share it. Pepsi didn't change any aspect of their beverage for United Airlines. However, the conversation they had about it was tailored to the individual with whom they had it.

Fifty Shades of Gray

Imagine you sell copiers and your company's research and development team has just shared a major announcement. "We have just developed the first copier in the world that prints fifty shades of gray. No other company can print that number of shades of this color." Everyone in the company is excited about the new copier and feels it's going to be a game changer.

This morning, you have a meeting with a CFO to discuss this new copier. Will you be talking about the *fifty shades of gray* with him? I sure hope not—for so many reasons. Most important, you wouldn't have that conversation with the CFO because he doesn't care about colors, shades, and hues. What is important to a CFO is return on investment (ROI), cost reduction, and efficiency. The sales differentiation strategy with the CFO would be focused on the ways in which this new copier impacts those aspects.

Over lunch, you have a meeting with the marketing manager to discuss this new copier. She cares about print quality and speed, which makes those aspects effective message points. Her primary interests are probably not ROI, cost reduction, and efficiency, so it is not relevant to position those.

This afternoon, you have a meeting with the IT network manager regarding the copier. He doesn't care about print quality and speed nor does he care about ROI and efficiency. He is focused on copier reliability, network integration, and security. To win the deal at the prices you want, the meeting with him needs to be focused on those three aspects, as that is the conversation he will be interested in having.

I've just described three meetings regarding the same product, but the sales differentiation conversation during those meetings is completely different given each person's interests. Just like the Pepsi example, no aspect of the copier was changed. What did change is the way in which the salesperson positioned the solution for each DI.

Buyer Engagement

A client of mine had its salespeople deliver the same elevator story to all DIs. It didn't matter who you were or what your responsibilities were; you heard the same exact message. We conducted an analysis of the decision process for what the company sells and identified seventeen DIs. There was the potential that seventeen people, in different roles, would need to turn their keys for the deal to happen. Given their sales model, the company had (at best) a one in seventeen chance of hitting the mark with those DIs. We went through the process I just described and developed a set of elevator stories with messaging for each DI that aligned with their respective interests.

> **Before sharing "what you do" with a DI, take a moment to think about the person with whom you are about to share it.**

Your Decision Influencers

How can you put this into practice? In the last chapter, you went through an exercise whereby you prepared a list of your DIs. In the copier example, those people are the CFO, marketing manager, and IT network manager.

You were then tasked with two introspective questions to ask about each one of them. As each lies in bed at night thinking about his role and responsibilities, what is keeping the DI awake? Given what your company offers, how can you help the DIs address their individual concerns and objectives?

Based on what is keeping each DI up at night, position the relevant differentiators you possess in elevator stories. Notice the use of the word "relevant" before differentiators. For each differentiator you plan to align with a DI, make sure it is one that will resonate with that person. For the CFO, this is the set of differentiators that are financial in nature. The print quality and speed differentiators are the ones to position with the marketing manager. The IT network manager hears about the technology differentiators.

Your Target Client Profile

When you went through that exercise, it also became apparent for which Decision Influencers you have the strongest sales differentiation opportunities. That information is important to your selling effectiveness, as it affects your points of entry into an account. For example, if your strongest differentiators are cost reduction related, the ideal point of entry into the account would be those whose primary interests are financial, such as the CEO, CFO, or president. If your strongest differentiators are safety-related, those who are responsible for workplace injuries and safety are the ideal points of entry into the account.

There may also be circumstances when your sales differentiation strategy will not resonate at all. There's an old expression in sales that says: if you are going to lose, lose early. The idea behind that message is to minimize time and monetary investment in deals that you are not likely to win. A component of your sales differentiation strategy is the development of your target client profile. The purpose of that tool is to gain clarity around the accounts and opportunities (in addition to the DIs) where your sales differentiation strategy is most likely to hit the mark.

Many companies put together a 10,000-foot view of their ideal client, which makes for a great metaphor. Can you hit a target from 10,000 feet away? I'm guessing you probably can't and neither can your salespeople. Plus, the word "ideal" infers that it is a description of the perfect client, a one in a million account, rather than the specific type of accounts that they are most likely to win at desired price points. Salespeople need clarity for their sales pursuits. They need a detailed, target client profile so they aren't wasting valuable sales time chasing deals they can't win at the prices you want.

Here are nine aspects to address in your target client profile.

1. **Size.** Every industry and company has its own way of defining size. Some examples are annual revenue, number of employees, number of hires, number of locations, and growth rate. This is addressed in the profile to prevent your salespeople from pursuing deals that are too big or small relative to your sales differentiation strategy. The profile should address size in terms of range (5,000–10,000 employees) using metrics that are meaningful for and quantifiable to your type of sale. For example, if you sell human resources services, the number of employees is an element to be sure to address as it affects scope and pricing.

2. **Location.** Geography is another important component of the profile. Consider areas where your presence is stronger or ones in which you desire more clients. This could take into account your headquarters location, distribution centers, and satellite offices relative to where your target accounts are located. Examples of location include specific towns, cities, states, regions, and nations.

3. **Business type.** This considers their industry, which can be identified using NAICS (North American Industry Classification System) codes. The question to ask yourself is whether your solution resonates most with a specific industry or business type. If so, this is an important component to include in your profile.

4. **Incumbent.** If you know that some providers offer an inferior solution to yours, this could be an important component to consider. Another consideration is if you know there is a dynamic such as a service

issue or an acquisition that is affecting a provider's satisfaction level with clients. This component directs your salespeople to pursue accounts that use providers with these issues.

5. **Circumstances or goals.** To identify circumstances or goals, start sentences with the following expressions: "Our target client has issues with ... a desire to ... has the following compliance objectives ... has these management priorities ..." Some examples of circumstances or goals are to increase efficiency, reduce cost, drive growth, become scalable, improve process, reduce risk or liability, improve quality, and acquire data. This component helps a salesperson to identify relevant differentiators for positioning, during both pre-call preparation and the meeting.

6. **Decision drivers.** These are drivers that raise awareness of the solutions you provide and create an environment in which a buyer would be motivated to make a change. For example, if you sell home security systems, decision drivers are the purchase of a new home or a crime increase in a neighborhood. Some examples of decision drivers within a company are a new executive being hired, an acquisition, the launch of a new product, the opening of a new location, a workforce reduction, a fine, a lawsuit, and regulatory changes.

7. **Corporate attributes.** This component addresses corporate DNA—elements such as financial health, defined corporate objectives, and company culture. If your solution requires financing through your company (credit), the financial health of the buyer is an example of an attribute you will want to address. Credit worthiness means that you will want to contrast your requirements with their financials before investing sales time pursuing the account.

8. **Buying process.** Not every company buys or makes decisions in a way that is aligned with *WHAT you sell's* meaningful value. First, identify the departments that you desire to be most influential in driving the decision-making process. If your sales differentiation strategy resonates most with CFOs, include senior financial executives in the profile.

Second, address the process they use to purchase. If they only buy through a formal request for proposal (RFP) and you are not a low-price provider, there is a decreased likelihood of winning the deal at the prices you want.

Another consideration for this component is whether someone is already looking for a solution (an active buyer) versus you inspiring the buyer to consider an alternative (a passive buyer). Some sales differentiation strategies are more effective with informed, educated, active buyers while others are more effective when the salesperson is the one motivating the buyer to explore change.

9. **Dealbreakers.** This component is the converse of the target client. Dealbreakers are aspects that you do not want. They include slow payer, financial issues, poor rating, wants kickbacks, bad reputation, not in the geography in which you operate, etc. You certainly don't want salespeople wasting time chasing deals you don't want or can't win at the prices you want.

By developing this profile, you avoid salespeople wasting countless hours pursuing deals where your sales differentiation strategy isn't likely to resonate with DIs. This tool provides salespeople with a laser-focus for their selling efforts, so they aren't pursuing the wrong deals while your competitors win the right ones.

Knowing which accounts and DIs are most likely to be interested in exploring relationships with your company and having differentiated messaging aligned with their interests are key elements of your sales differentiation strategy.

SALES DIFFERENTIATION CONCEPT #6

Not all differentiators matter to all Decision Influencers or in all circumstances.

CHAPTER 7

ARE YOU LEAVING DIFFERENTIATION OPEN TO BUYER INTERPRETATION?

If you recruit salespeople and want to see an instant smile appear on their faces, tell them you are the biggest player in your industry. Salespeople perceive "biggest" as a powerful, standout differentiator. Salespeople and, truth be told, executives puff out their chests when they say they are the largest provider. And why shouldn't they? Being the biggest makes you the premier player.

But let's turn this around. Try recruiting salespeople with the opening statement that you are the smallest player in the industry. Most sales candidates will be turned off because they infer the company is weak, novice, and unstable.

In both of these examples, the salespeople (who are the buyers in this case) derive meaning from the presented differentiator. That meaning was left to them to define and decide how they felt about it. This created an overall perception for the buyer that the seller failed to manage.

"Biggest"—Blessing or Curse?

Being the biggest may make salespeople and executives boastful, but this differentiator is not necessarily meaningful to buyers. It's not uncommon to find several companies in an industry touting that they are the biggest. The first question is how they define "biggest." Does the company have the highest revenue, profits, number of employees, or number of clients? It's not uncommon to find multiple providers within an industry saying they are the largest because there are many ways to define it.

Before getting too excited about anchoring your sales differentiation strategy to your company's size, think about the second question that is more important.

Why does size matter to my buyers?

If you leave the meaning of the differentiator for the buyers to determine, they might not view size as positively as you do. Here are four examples (Figure 7-1) of "biggest" and how buyers could potentially perceive them if a salesperson doesn't provide context.

FIGURE 7-1: Differentiator Shared without Context

DIFFERENTIATOR	POTENTIAL BUYER CONCERNS
Most revenue	"Did they grow through acquisition? Integrating companies is challenging and clients suffer from it. I don't want to work with a company like that."
Most profitable	"Are they driving profitability by making nominal investments in operations, technology, and service? I don't want to work with a company like that."
Most clients	"Am I just going to be a number to this company? I don't want to work with a company like that."
Most employees	"Are the competitors using technology more efficiently and cost-effectively? I don't want to work with a company like that."

In each of those cases, the salesperson has lobbed a differentiator at a buyer and left defining its meaning to the buyer. Let's try this exercise again. This time the salesperson gives context to the differentiator creating buyer intrigue rather than concern (Figure 7-2).

Figure 7-2: Differentiator Shared with Context

DIFFERENTIATOR	DIFFERENTIATOR CONTEXT PROVIDED
Most revenue	"Our size gives us strong buying power which reduces costs for our clients."
Most profitable	"We are continually reinvesting in the business to ensure we delight our clients each and every day."
Most clients	"We have well-defined processes supported by technology so that every client feels as if they are our only one."
Most employees	"We recognize service is very important to our clients. Technology only gets you so far. We use technology where it makes sense. We also have identified places in our process for well-trained employees as that is what will delight our clients."

So, is "biggest" a blessing or a curse? The answer is entirely based on how that differentiator has been positioned by the salesperson. While "biggest" has its advantages, "smaller" has its benefits as well. If you are selling for a smaller company, you could position your size as beneficial to a buyer for you are nimble and flexible. You can provide personalized attention to the account that a larger provider cannot. And, clients have more access to the management team.

By giving context to the differentiator, its value has been positioned and "definition-risk" removed from the equation. If you leave defining differentiator meaning to your DIs, you will get one of two results. Either they will never figure out why it matters, or they will give it a meaning that you aren't going to like. On their own, Decision Influencers will never give a differentiator context that is advantageous to you. If you leave setting differentiator context to them, you will lose. Guaranteed!

> Decision Influencers will never give a differentiator context that is advantageous to you. If you leave setting differentiator context to them, you will lose. Guaranteed!

The "Local" Differentiator

A major U.S.-based company was having sales differentiation challenges in other countries in which they operate. In its industry, this company is not only the largest provider of the services they offer in the U.S., but in other countries as well. In the U.S., the salespeople anchored their sales differentiation strategy on "biggest" and it worked, given the context in which they gave it. Outside the U.S., however, they faced fierce competition from several providers headquartered within those other countries. The competition was kicking their butts when an executive reached out to me for help.

When competing against this company, each of those competitors differentiated themselves as the "local provider" and gave DIs reasons why they should buy local, such as that it supported the local economy. The strategy was effective and caused the U.S.-based company to cut prices in those countries to keep existing clients and win new deals. Something needed to change and fast.

Upon hearing this story, I asked the division president of one of these countries how many employees his company had in that country. He responded, "Over ten thousand." This U.S.-based company had created more than ten thousand jobs for citizens living in that country. How many employees did the local competitor have? The executive responded, "If you added the number of in-country employees for all of the local competitors in the country, it is a fraction of the total number of employees that we have." In other words, the number of in-country employees the U.S.-based company had was significantly more than all their local competitors combined.

While the locally owned competitors positioned that buying from them supported the local economy, which company was contributing more to that purpose? Most of the dollars paid to the U.S.-based company's ten thousand employees were being spent locally—in that country.

Back to the question, which company was helping the local economy more? The answer may seem obvious now, but the positioning of that differentiator had been completely missed by both the executives and the salespeople. They had left the meaning of "biggest" open to buyer interpretation and left themselves vulnerable to competition.

After our conversation, this company turned the sales differentiation tables on its competitors. The U.S.-based company was truly the right local option for supporting the country's economic growth. Rather than simply stating that they were the biggest, they positioned the local economic impact of buying from them. This quickly turned the sales tide and they no longer were fighting to win deals based on price.

"Waste" Opportunity

A Minnesota company in the waste industry (i.e., garbage) was searching for a sales differentiation strategy. In this state, most counties and cities leave contracting for trash service up to homeowners and business owners. Every Wednesday, there is a parade of garbage trucks, representing all the different haulers, driving through my neighborhood, seemingly performing the same tasks. The truck drives up to a home and extends a mechanical arm that lifts the trash can. The can is emptied into the truck and placed back on the driveway, the truck drives away, and the homeowner receives an invoice at the end of the month for services rendered.

The CEO of one of these companies felt that its services provided meaningful value to its clientele, which justified a higher price point, but the company's salespeople didn't know how to position it. During a brain-share session with the team, I asked them to share a differentiator they position with Decision Influencers. The first one offered was "privately held," to which I asked why that mattered to a DI. No one could answer my question, so I challenged the team.

"For thirty-plus years, you've been touting to buyers that you are privately held, expecting it to be meaningful, but none of you can tell me why that matters to them."

They began talking among themselves. "We should stop talking about being privately held."

I challenged them again. I asked how many of them had worked for a publicly traded company at some point in their careers. Half of the group had. "In those companies, what was the number one priority?" In unison, they shouted, "The numbers!" I agreed. If you are the head of customer service in a publicly traded company and want to add five people more than what was budgeted for, it takes an act from a divine being to get it approved because that cost distorts the company's financials.

"What about in a privately held company? The number one priority is what?" I asked. Again, in unison, but boisterously this time, they responded, "The clients!" A knowing look appeared on their faces as they saw there was a differentiated story to position based on being privately held, and we worked together to flesh it out.

I asked the group for another differentiator they shared with DIs. This time they said, "Locally owned and operated." Why did that matter? Again, no one in the room could tell me. At that point, I told the group that I wasn't originally from Minnesota. I looked at them and said, "This is the screwiest climate on the planet." They chuckled, but I was serious. If you perform a Google search for the places in the world that can have the most extreme temperatures in a single calendar year, many of those cities are in Minnesota. Few places on the planet have temperatures that range from above one hundred degrees Fahrenheit to below negative twenty-five degrees Fahrenheit in a twelve-month period. Yet, that's exactly what the weather is like in the Minneapolis suburb where I live.

Stepping back, I asked the group to remind me what business they were in. They said, "The garbage business." I quickly corrected them. "Not true. You are in the trucking business. And what do trucks hate?" Trucks don't perform well in extreme cold or hot temperatures. They falter in severe heat and cold.

Just then, their operations manager raised his hand. "Last year," he said, "our company was the only one in the state [in the waste hauling industry] not to miss one day of service due to weather." The salespeople almost fell out of their chairs. Unaware of this feat, they were shocked.

They also had completely misunderstood their differentiator. By being locally owned and operated, the company had developed an expertise in providing services in a very difficult climate. Certainly, no DI ever understood "locally owned and operated" to mean this. Again, if you don't give the differentiator meaning, DIs will either never figure it out or define it in a way that does not help your sale.

American Strength

A fitness equipment company touted that they were an American manufacturer. When asked why that mattered to a buyer, their salespeople proudly shared altruistic responses. "We should all support American-manufactured brands," they said. While altruism is a component of the differentiator's meaning, there was a bigger story that was not being positioned with buyers.

Most of the company's competitors manufactured equipment in China. Given the size and weight of the equipment, it could only be transported one way from China to the United States. That was by ship. That meant it would take several months to receive an order. This U.S. manufacturer, however, could turn it around in a matter of weeks. Any buyer who wanted their fitness equipment quickly had to buy from an American manufacturer of which there were few.

The salespeople had focused on the altruistic story and not positioned "order speed," which turned out to be the stronger differentiator message with Decision Influencers.

Regardless of the differentiators you possess, never leave the context of those to buyer interpretation. If you leave it to their interpretation, you lose all control of the true value of your differentiator and the deal. For each differentiator you are going to position, ask yourself why it should matter to the buyer. If you can't answer why, perhaps this differentiator should not be shared.

SALES DIFFERENTIATION CONCEPT #7

Sales differentiation requires the salesperson to position why it matters to the buyer.

CHAPTER 8

WHOSE FAULT IS IT
WHEN A BUYER DOESN'T SEE YOUR
DIFFERENTIATED VALUE?

As I mentioned in Chapter 7, I live in a Minneapolis suburb. However, I'm not originally from Minnesota. I grew up in New York City and New Jersey. When I shared the story of the garbage truck company with you, I mentioned the brutally cold winters we have in Minnesota. It's not uncommon to have winters with temperatures colder than minus twenty degrees with wind chills below negative fifty degrees. In some years, we experience subzero temperatures the entire month of January. Coming from the East Coast, I've discovered an entirely new definition for the expression "cold winters."

Of course, what comes with cold temperatures? Snow . . . from November through May—and plenty of it. Minnesotans celebrate the arrival of snow. My neighbors will be out, not only snowblowing their own driveways, but also enjoying being out in the elements. They enjoy it so much that, once they remove snow from their property, they look for other driveways and sidewalks to clear. They have "Minnesota skin" which enables them to enjoy the brutally cold temperatures. Not me. I have "East Coast skin." East Coasters are not accustomed to this level of cold. When you relocate here, like I did, you aren't issued "Minnesota skin."

I shared how Minnesotans handle snow. However, people who are from the New York City area deal with snow differently. We don't clear snow ourselves, but rather we get "a guy" to do it for us. I have no interest in pushing around a snowblower in this climate which means I had to find "a guy" to do it.

Snow Job

I went online and found a website that connects homeowners with contractors offering a variety of services including snow removal. I filled out the interest form which the website then sent to five contractors for consideration. The scope of the service I needed was simply to remove snow from my driveway, sidewalk, and front door walkway. There was nothing unique or special about my requirements.

After I submitted the form, one of the contractors sent me an email and we exchanged some pleasantries since we both live in the same Minneapolis suburb. He seemed like a good guy and I was hoping to use his company's services.

A day went by and the website notified me that all five contractors had submitted their bids for this project. When I logged in and reviewed their pricing, I got sticker shock from that contractor's bid. He was more expensive than the others—not a little more, but significantly more. I was disappointed because given the email conversation we had, I was planning to use his company. In my mind, I couldn't justify using his firm given the delta between his prices and all the others. After all, the task is just removing snow from around my home. What could possibly justify his price?

Given my concern about his pricing, I sent a polite, one sentence email to him that said, "I wish your price was lower." That's all my email said. Here is his email response to it:

> "With my company you get what you pay for. Quality and reliability have a cost. I have new, well-maintained equipment that costs well over one hundred thousand dollars. Also, I am fully

insured and can send you a certificate of insurance if you like from my agent's office. If you want cheap, I am not it. I charge reasonable prices for good services. That's why I have been in business twenty-five plus years."

Great Response or Not?

When I talk about sales differentiation philosophy I share this story with audiences and ask their opinion of his emailed response. Most nod and smile. They think his response is fantastic. That's when I share there are five missteps within it.

First, he tossed out expressions like "quality" and "reliability." What did he mean by "quality?" All he was being asked to do was remove snow from a driveway, walkway, and sidewalk. A ten-dollar shovel from Home Depot gets the job done. What is "quality" with this type of project? I have no idea what he meant by the word, as he left it to me to decipher its meaning.

"Reliability" is interesting. My wife works at the high school that my kids attend. Was he saying he would have the snow removed before they needed to leave for school? I would pay more for that service. I don't know what he meant by "reliability." Again, it was left for me to figure out. As I shared earlier, when you rely on your DI to give a differentiator context, one of two things will happen: Either he doesn't figure it out or he gives it a meaning that is not advantageous to you. Every time you share a differentiator, it's critical to explain why it matters to this individual. In this case, I never figured out what was meant by either of those expressions.

Second, he mentioned having equipment that costs well over a hundred thousand dollars. I respect what he was trying to accomplish. He was attempting to differentiate himself by showing he had invested in the business. But as I said, a ten-dollar shovel gets the job done.

That "hundred thousand dollars" statement got me thinking. Maybe his primary business is commercial which requires this type of equipment, and he is dabbling in the residential market. This would explain why his price is so much higher. In other words, it seemed like he didn't have the right equipment for this job. Not only is it a key to give a differentiator context, but also to consider how the buyer could receive it. To flip the coin, a hundred thousand dollars is not that much money for snow removal equipment. That investment covers the cost of two pickup trucks with plows.

Next, half of his email talks about the insurance coverage he has. That was another flawed differentiation strategy. I wasn't thinking about damage to my home, but I am now. Given the tenor of the email, it made me wonder if he has had problems in the past with damaging residential properties while removing snow. As I stated in my point about his equipment investment, be mindful of how your differentiator could be perceived by a buyer.

Fourth, the tone of the email is very defensive. "With my company you get what you pay for." "If you want cheap, I am not it." In other words, it's my fault that I don't perceive meaningful value in the services he provides, and therefore he is angry with me. Salespeople need to take ownership of a DI perceiving meaningful differentiation. It's never the DI's fault when she doesn't see a material difference to justify a higher price. It's yours.

> It's never the DI's fault when he doesn't see a material difference to justify a higher price. It's yours.

Finally, given that his price was so much higher than the other contractors, this could not have been the first time he received feedback that his pricing was out of line. Rather than address it proactively, he crossed his fingers and hoped it did not become an issue. As I shared earlier, you can never be too early when it comes to differentiation, but you can be too late. Waiting for price to become an issue makes it nearly impossible to differentiate yourself and save the deal.

Still think his response was fantastic?

During a client presentation, I shared this story and the issues associated with the email response. Later in the day, the company's CEO took me aside during a break and said, "When you first presented the contractor's email, I was in the group that thought it was perfect. Quite frankly, I've written very similar emails. Now seeing those five issues, I will never respond that way again."

Saving the Deal

After I share the issues with this contractor's response, I ask my audiences to craft a better email message. I'll watch as they contemplate every word given how I dissected the prior one. After a few moments, I ask for volunteers to share their approach. After several of them do, I reveal that the exercise was actually a trick with an important point. The only thing they could have written in an email that would have affected the DI's decision was to offer to lower the price and match the other contractors. Other than that, the only strategy that would have potentially saved this deal was to pick up the phone and talk with the buyer.

Our email exchange was also a missed opportunity for him since I had never contracted for this type of service before. Maybe there were questions I should have been asking of contractors to make the right decision. Those questions may have explained why his price was so much higher.

While he should have differentiated himself at the beginning, he may have been able to recover if he had positioned his differentiators, on the phone or in-person, in a conversation like this:

> "I recognize that most homeowners have not contracted for snow removal services before. Would it be okay if I share with you some things to look for when making your decision?
>
> "Our industry runs the gamut from professionals like us to teenagers who slap a plow on their pickup truck and clear snow. One of the things homeowners often neglect to ask about when hiring a snow removal contractor is insurance. Removing snow and ice can be hazardous.

"I noticed that you have a basketball hoop on the side of your driveway. I don't expect we would have issues clearing snow from your home, but if there were to be an accident, like knocking into the hoop, we have the proper insurance to handle that. Not every snow removal provider has the right insurance for this type of work, so I encourage you to ask about that when evaluating service providers, or it could become your financial responsibility in the event something goes wrong."

From there, he could have inquired about my needs such as having the snow removed before my wife and kids needed to leave for school. That would have given him an opportunity to differentiate himself by committing to clear it before they needed to back out of the garage. He could have also talked about his drivers' expertise and their safety record in removing snow from homes.

Unfortunately for him, he never picked up the phone. His email to me was our last communication and he lost the deal. While most salespeople become angry when DIs push back on price, take an alternative perspective. Recognize it as constructive criticism with an opportunity to revisit your sales differentiation strategy. Take ownership of the fact they don't see meaningful value in what you have shared and retool your communication strategy.

SALES DIFFERENTIATION CONCEPT #8

The ownership of a buyer perceiving differentiation resides with you, the salesperson.

II.

HOW
YOU SELL

CHAPTER 9

DIFFERENTIATING THROUGH YOUR SELLING APPROACH

When I first introduce the subject of differentiation to salespeople, they immediately point their fingers at their employers. "It is their job to create a differentiated product for us to sell at the prices they want." In the minds of salespeople, differentiation is the company's responsibility. They are partially right. Certainly, a company has a responsibility to create a differentiated offering that justifies the price they've assigned to it. However, what salespeople often fail to realize is the tremendous opportunity to differentiate beyond the features and functions of *WHAT you sell*. That opportunity resides in *HOW you sell*.

In the prior chapters of the book, we explored ways to differentiate *WHAT you sell*. Yet, there is only so much a product, service, or technology can be differentiated. Salespeople are expected to win deals at the company's desired price points based on what they have been given in their bag to sell. That limitation leads to frustration because salespeople usually can't make what they sell bigger, smaller, redder, bluer, rounder, or squarer. They have to sell what it is.

What happens when what you are selling is identical or very similar to what the competition has to offer? How do you win more deals at desired price points? The answer is to use *HOW you sell* to create meaningful differentiation such that Decision Influencers prefer to buy from you instead of the competition.

The Ring

On July 24, 1996, I proposed to my then girlfriend, Sharon, in the White House Rose Garden. I'll never forget all the emotions I was feeling leading to that special moment. In particular, I remember the excitement and concerns I had regarding the purchase of a diamond engagement ring. Not leaving anything to chance, since Sharon and I had already talked about getting married, I included her in the process of buying this special ring.

There are many places where you can buy an engagement ring, but what was the right place for us? I had never purchased a ring like this before, nor had I spent the amount of money I was about to spend on a piece of jewelry. I was concerned about not knowing the questions to ask to make an informed decision. Back then, I didn't have the robust internet that exists today to seek guidance. Friends of mine who had already been through the engagement ring purchase process shared the basics about diamond quality, color, clarity, etc., but I was sure there were other important considerations when making this purchase. Like most people going through this experience for the first time, I was what you would describe as an uneducated buyer.

We were living in the D.C. Metro area at the time. I came across a jewelry store that is well known for diamond engagement rings. Were their diamonds of a better quality than what other stores sold? I'm guessing they weren't. But they differentiated themselves in the way they sold their stones and ring settings, which led us to buy from them.

First of all, we couldn't just walk into the store and look at engagement rings. An appointment was required for a consultation with a salesperson. When we arrived for our scheduled appointment, we didn't meet in a big showroom with extensive ring choices as well as other ring buyers milling about. We were taken to a private room that had nothing in it other than comfortable chairs and a fancy desk. This initially struck us as odd because other jewelry stores displayed rings everywhere you looked, but this quickly developed into a very effective sales differentiation strategy.

Before beginning the conversation about rings, we were offered a glass of wine. As the consultation began, the salesperson asked us a series of questions to understand our perspective on engagement rings and the knowledge we had in purchasing diamonds. Only after that conversation with the salesperson was completed were we offered the opportunity to see stones and ring settings. This too was vastly different from other jewelry stores, which displayed a ring with a stone already set in it. This store separated the components of the ring into two distinct decision steps. Based on our responses to her questions, the saleswoman showed us the stones and rings that would be of greatest interest to us. This personalized the experience and saved us a lot of time.

Most important, the salesperson clearly understood how we were feeling at that time. She shared our excitement about this momentous occasion and appreciated all the other emotions, concerns, and fears that went along with it. I remember thinking that she understood us, which was very meaningful in our decision-making process.

I'm sure we could have purchased a less costly ring elsewhere, but this sales experience made us comfortable and confident in our purchasing decision. We knew that this was the right company for us. And this salesperson was the one from whom we wanted to make this purchase. The sales experience was the difference maker!

Pulling the Rug Out From Under Us

My wife and I decided to replace the carpet in our dining room. We had been in our home about fourteen years and it was already carpeted when we bought it. We definitely fell into the category of "uneducated buyer for carpeting." We first went to a large home retailer to purchase new carpet and were overwhelmed by our choices. No one offered to assist us, so I walked up to one of the salespeople and asked for help.

He pointed to a few carpet samples, smiled, and walked away. He was very nice but provided no value in helping us with decision-making. As you can probably surmise, we didn't purchase anything and left the store frustrated. We had gone there intent on buying but became overwhelmed by the number of choices and the lack of decision guidance. That store lost a deal.

As we drove home, we passed by a flooring retail store and decided to try our luck again. We walked in and, just as with the large home retailer, we were overwhelmed by all the carpet choices. But we didn't feel that way for long.

A salesperson came up to us shortly after we walked into the store and asked a few questions. Our answers reduced the seemingly unlimited and overwhelming options down to a select few. She stayed with us throughout the entire decision process and helped us make the right choice. Thus, we bought from her.

Was their carpet any better than the other store? I don't believe there was any difference between the two stores or their selection of merchandise. Was their price lower? I probably paid a little more at this store, but I didn't care. The way this salesperson helped us buy made the difference for us. The selling experience provided meaningful value.

It's the job of salespeople to help people buy.

Throughout this book, I've shared stories highlighting the point that people don't know how to buy what you sell. This creates an opportunity and an obligation for salespeople. The opportunity resides in your helping shape buyer decision criteria, so they make the right decision for themselves. The obligation component comes into play because one of the core responsibilities of the sales function is to help people make informed buying decisions. It's the job of salespeople to help people buy.

Best Price

The new car industry has embraced *HOW you sell* to differentiate the car purchase experience for a buyer. Most people would prefer root canal to buying a car. Buying a car is not perceived as a pleasant experience. The most dreaded part is price negotiation. Some dealerships, recognizing that point, changed the way in which they sell.

They present their best price for the car upfront with no negotiation (or "haggle" as they describe it) whatsoever. People who want to avoid the negotiation headache will elect to buy from these dealerships. They may pay a few more dollars, but they feel it is worth it to avoid sales stress. For them, "no haggling" translates to differentiated, meaningful value.

Differentiating Commodity

Every phase of the sales process presents the opportunity to create meaningful differentiation. From the first phone call to a prospect, to an RFP response, to the request for references, there are opportunities to be different from the competition—and those differences become the reasons why someone buys from you.

In the employment background screening industry, background checks are a commodity. Often the same data sources and researchers conduct the analyses for multiple background screening providers. In most cases, if you order the same background check scope from any of these providers for a candidate, the reports will be identical.

In the 1990s and early 2000s, many of these screening providers' selling strategy was to offer to save employers a small percentage on their employment background screening program. "What if we could save you 5 percent on your screening program?" That was their way of getting in the

Every phase of the sales process presents the opportunity to create meaningful differentiation.

door. The net result was a marketplace that didn't see a difference among providers. Consequently, price became the primary decision point.

The background-screening provider for which I was the chief sales officer had no interest in battling over pricing for table scrap deals. The industry's approach was eroding margins and that model was unacceptable to us. However, it was impossible to differentiate each background check due to the commoditized perception of them (which was reinforced by the industry's selling strategy). Rather than fight the price battle, we developed our sales differentiation strategy around two main points that were important to buyers.

We found those two by introspectively asking why companies performed this type of screening. The answer was "to make informed hiring decisions fast." Both accuracy and speed of this verification process were very important to most employers.

While our competitors focused their DI meetings on the price of the checks, we taught our salespeople to analyze the entire hiring process in search of opportunities to reduce their time-to-hire cycle. Our salespeople were successful at identifying opportunities for improvement which gave executives the perception (and rightfully so) that we had expertise in hiring process management.

Second, we recognized that we had a greater expertise in the design of an employment screening solution than those to whom we were selling. Most executives had no idea why their program was structured the way that it was. Our salespeople helped them craft background screening programs based on their hiring profile to cost-effectively reduce their risk.

This strategy led us to have consistent year-over-year revenue growth in excess of 30 percent for several years and to be recognized by *Inc.* magazine for our growth accomplishments. We positioned expertise and differentiated *HOW you sell* to create meaningful value. Our salespeople did not have the ability to change the scope of the background checks or the way they were performed. Thus, our approach was to differentiate *HOW you sell* to win more deals at the prices we wanted. And it worked!

Differentiating Proposals

There was a third way our background screening company used *HOW you sell* as a differentiator. We also differentiated ourselves in how we presented our solution and pricing. Our competitors delivered theirs in massive, colorful documents that were mostly marketing fluff. Because of the nature of the commoditization of those background checks, while the color and layout of the document may have been different from provider to provider, the content was mostly the same.

To further differentiate ourselves in *HOW you sell*, we didn't send a pretty, colorful proposal to present our solution. We told our DIs that we would produce a statement of work for them that articulated how we would deliver services and manage their accounts. Marketing fluff was absent from our document as we told them it would be. There was no color and there were no photos in our statement of work. We told them that they could read all the marketing information about our company on our website. The statement of work was a document they could hold in their hands and know exactly what they were getting for their investment.

Buyers often told us that they found our approach refreshing and commented that no one else in our industry conducted business the way we did. While our background checks were very similar to our competitors, we created meaningful differentiation with *HOW you sell*.

I continue to use statements of work when selling my sales management consulting services. I treat it as a technical document that shows the deliverables associated with the engagement. If someone wants to learn more about me, my website is chock-full. Clients regularly tell me that I'm the only one they've come across who uses this approach. Differentation mission accomplished!

Do It Yourself . . . With Help

Even in retail sales, there is an opportunity to use *HOW you sell* to create meaningful value. Home Depot sells the same products as other home-building retailers. The company developed a strategy to provide meaningful value intended to attract the do-it-yourself homeowner to their stores. Home Depot did this with its staffing model.

While its competitors hired typical retail, hourly employees, Home Depot hired professional craftsmen. I remember when I was a kid, my father saying he was going to Home Depot to talk with a plumber. Home Depot hired plumbers, electricians, and other professional craftsmen to help "do-it-yourselfers" that came into the store. They saw Home Depot as a source for expertise, went there for guidance, and subsequently bought there. What Home Depot sold wasn't different from other home-building retailers, but how they sold it was.

The balance of this book teaches you ways to provide meaningful, differentiated value in *HOW you sell*. You'll learn how to differentiate yourself from the initial contact all the way through a DI's request for references—and every step in between. You'll even learn ways to differentiate yourself based on the way you handle buyer objections. These lessons are shared with you with the fundamental goal of winning more deals at the prices you want.

SALES DIFFERENTIATION CONCEPT #9

HOW you sell, not just *WHAT you sell*, differentiates you.

CHAPTER 10

ALIGNING YOUR SALES DIFFERENTIATION STRATEGY WITH DECISION INFLUENCERS

Years ago, a company recruited me to build a sales team tasked with selling products identical to our competition, but at a premium price. In other words, this team would be selling the same offering as our competitors but would be expected to get more money for it. When the CEO first approached me about the "opportunity," I thought I was being "punked," but he was dead serious. While some of my friends thought I was crazy for considering this role, I accepted the challenge and took on this executive sales leadership position.

This was during the dot-com boom when software powerhouses like Microsoft, Novell, and IBM were seemingly releasing new software monthly. After many years of developing software, executives from these companies came to realize that if they didn't offer training on the proper use of their software, the likelihood that users would purchase upgrades or buy additional products from them was slim. They recognized that they needed high levels of product user satisfaction to drive future sales.

Not only was there a user satisfaction concern to address, there was also a major shortage of skilled IT workers in the industry. That personnel limitation impeded the software companies' sales growth. If their clients couldn't hire skilled workers or train employees themselves, they would be unable to deploy the new software.

Most of these software companies also realized that "training" was not among their core competencies, nor were they interested in developing it. Instead they elected to develop a training channel comprised of individual training companies and small training networks. Those contractual relationships had a variety of designations; however, they were commonly referred to as "authorized training partners."

While the software companies didn't want to enter the training delivery business directly, they also saw the prudence of controlling the learning environment. They didn't let their network of trainers determine how to educate in the proper use of the software products. The software companies controlled the learning environment.

Being Commoditized by Our Partners

The software companies set a goal of creating a "McDonald's experience" for their education. That meant that someone could attend training at any of their authorized training partners' facilities and have the same outstanding experience.

To accomplish that goal, the authorized training partners were required to exclusively use the course materials that the software companies developed. Only their certified instructors were permitted to teach the courses. They also regulated class size and specified the hardware and software requirements for each student's computer. Again, the software companies' goal was to create a vanilla learning experience, so they could boast of having thousands of training facilities delivering product education on their behalf.

While the software companies wanted to create commodity, the training channel fought that philosophy. Each one of them wanted to get top dollar for their training, as most of the software companies left course price setting up to their partners' discretion.

Getting Inside the Minds of Our Buyers

This was the challenge I accepted—to build a sales force that would sell these same technology-training courses at higher prices than our competitors. We were expected to win deals at those higher prices despite our competitors offering the same courses, using the same course materials delivered by certified instructors.

Course prices, among competitors, were all over the board. Many of our competitors preached that their training was the "best." Their salespeople called on IT managers and said, "We have the best training, the best instructors, and the latest PCs in the classrooms." This was their strategy to justify their course prices. How could they make a believable "best" claim given that the software companies controlled the classroom environment? The software companies who were preaching that all of us were the same certainly didn't reinforce it.

Taking it a step further, most of the course instructors were independent contractors. An instructor teaching for my company this month would likely be teaching for my competitor next month. Some instructors even taught for one training company during the day and another at night. Not surprisingly, IT managers quickly got wise to the lack of differentiation in the training courses, and the "best" strategy didn't work.

While our salespeople and I passionately believed that our training was superior to that offered by our competitors, we couldn't prove it to Decision Influencers considering the classroom control by the software companies. This necessitated development of a different strategy, given our "win more deals at the prices we want" objective. The software companies had turned the classroom into a commodity, but I firmly believed we still had an opportunity to provide meaningful value that people would pay more to have.

I brought my sales team together for a brain-share session to devise our sales differentiation strategy. I tasked them with a foundation question pertaining to the development of the strategy.

"What challenges do IT managers face with respect to IT training?"

After much discussion and whiteboarding, we identified three major IT manager frustrations. The first was the process to procure training for the IT manager's department. We learned that it took as many as five signatures on a purchase order to approve one person for a $1,500 course. It was burdensome and annoying for both the manager and employee. Frequently, the final approval needed to send someone for training was not received in time for the start of the course, which meant the employee could not attend the class.

These courses were not delivered every week; some were not delivered every month. Every day that the team was untrained was another day that the department was not fully equipped to support the technology. Each time the manager wanted to send someone for training, the same process was repeated. As one IT manager said, "it was a bureaucratic nightmare."

The second frustration was student satisfaction with the courses. When the IT manager finally received all the necessary approvals to send someone for training, he felt a sense of relief and accomplishment. When the employee returned from the program, the manager would greet her with a welcoming smile and excitement as there was now another skilled person to support the technology.

Oftentimes, the smile and excitement were short lived as the manager asked the employee about the course experience. "I thought I was going to learn about X and they taught me about Y, so this wasn't the right class for me." Or the employee would say, "I didn't realize there were prerequisites for the course. The content went right over my head." This employee had been out of the office for a week, if not several weeks, receiving training. Because of this issue, she was no further along in being able to work with the technology than she was before she attended the class and the company's training dollars were wasted.

Third, the IT manager would send someone for training who would come back, work for them for a few months, and quit because she obtained a more lucrative job resulting from these newly acquired skills.

The IT manager had wasted training dollars on an employee who was no longer on his team. The fact that this person left did not reset the manager's training budget. The dollars were lost forever. IT turnover was a very real issue during the dot-com boom. Some IT managers were so fearful of this issue that they avoided training their people on the new technology.

Sales Differentiation for a Commodity

Given these three major challenges plaguing IT managers, I tasked my team with developing a sales differentiation strategy such that IT managers would want to send their employees to us for training rather than the competition—at the prices we wanted. The goal of our sales differentiation strategy was to make it easier for IT managers to procure the right training for their teams and adeptly support the technology their companies had purchased.

Here's the three-part sales differentiation strategy we developed:

To help with the challenge of procuring training, we positioned the concept of a blanket purchase order (PO). We had learned that the purchase order approval process, in most companies, was the same for a $1,500 course as it was for a million dollars of training. The thought behind the blanket purchase order concept was for them to issue us a purchase order for their entire training budget for the year. We billed against it as they sent employees to courses, which created no risk to them. This allowed them to go through the laborious purchase order approval process once for the year rather than for each individual course.

In most cases, our salespeople had to engage directors, vice presidents, and chief information officers in the blanket purchase order conversation since most IT managers didn't have the authority to issue it. This also allowed us to expand our influence and develop relationships with other DIs, at higher levels, in the companies.

The blanket purchase order strategy also helped us lock out the competition. Once a PO for the year's training budget was issued to us, there was nothing a competitor could say or do to get in the door, other than offer free training.

Second, we took ownership of the student satisfaction issue. We put a policy in place that said we would issue a full credit, no questions asked, for a student who was dissatisfied with a class for any reason. This policy helped protect the IT manager's training budget but did not address the major problem associated with student satisfaction issues, which was a shortage of skilled employees to support the technology.

To address that point, we put in place a team of what we called "education advisors." Rather than allow a client's employees to enroll in courses by phone, fax, or online, they would be interviewed by an education advisor. The advisor's responsibility was to ensure every student was right for the course in which they were enrolling, and the course was right for the student. In other words, education advisors made sure the course provided the training the employee needed and that she had the background to succeed in it. We personalized the enrollment experience.

Finally, these companies needed budget protection for newly trained workers who left for a better paying job. To help with this, we offered a replacement guarantee. If an employee we trained left their company within six months of completing a course, we offered to train her replacement for just the price of the course materials (the books).

As a result of this sales differentiation strategy, we became one of the largest, most profitable training companies for Microsoft, Novell, and IBM/Lotus. Our salespeople were able to sell our "same courses" at 30 to 50 percent higher prices than our competitors. While our competitors argued "best," we positioned meaningful differentiation that aligned with what was most important to Decision Influencers.

There's an old business expression that says, "Think outside the box." For us, the classroom was our "box." Per our contract with the software companies, authorized training partners like us were prohibited from doing anything to differentiate ourselves through the learning experience. The product we were selling was unchangeable. The only opportunity we had to create meaningful differences was outside of the classroom.

Don't just look at *WHAT you sell* and its attributes as you develop your sales differentiation strategy. Consider the challenges frustrating your Decision Influencers and the ways in which you can help address them. The synergy between their frustrations and what you offer can be the foundation for an effective sales differentiation strategy.

> Consider the challenges frustrating your Decision Influencers and the ways in which you can help address them.

In an earlier chapter, you participated in a DI analysis exercise based on two questions. The answers to the questions exposed what was keeping DIs up at night and how you can help. Reflect on your "synergy" responses to identify opportunities you have in *HOW you sell.*

SALES DIFFERENTIATION CONCEPT #10

Sales differentiation is not limited by product attributes, but rather by the solutions that can be innovated to address buyer challenges.

CHAPTER 11

DEVELOPING A SALES CRIME THEORY

It's the middle of the night and there is a pounding on your front door. Bam! Bam! Bam! You scramble to put on your robe and rush downstairs to see who's there. You peer out the window and see flashing lights. It's the police! "We want to talk with you about a crime that was just committed."

How did the police come to arrive on your doorstep? Did they knock on every door in the neighborhood until they found someone to talk to? Of course, they didn't. They followed the trail of evidence and developed a crime theory. That crime theory led them to you for a conversation right now.

Could you imagine if the police force's crime resolution strategy was to go to every home and say "Hi, did you commit a crime today? If so, can you tell me which one, so we can close the case?" No suspects would ever be captured.

Making Buyers Miserable

While this isn't the police's strategy to find suspects, it is a very common sales practice. Salespeople blindly make calls hoping to find suspects that they can turn into prospects. If they can't find suspects, they can't turn them into prospects. No prospects means no sales. That's a sequence of events that even makes sense to Inspector Clouseau.

Not only is this approach painful for salespeople, it's a miserable experience for Decision Influencers. They receive random calls from salespeople saying what they have to offer is "best," who know nothing about them or their companies, and who fail to engage them in a meaningful way. Some polite DIs will tell you they are happy with their current provider and end the call. Others slam the phone down in disgust.

Believe it or not, most DIs have a target on them—a way to engage them such that they'll want to learn more about what you have to offer. Unfortunately, most salespeople handle prospecting calls in much the same way kids play pin the tail on the donkey: They blindly wander hoping to hit the target. It rarely worked at birthday parties and it rarely works in sales.

The Sales Crime Theory

What if we applied the police's crime-solving strategy to sales? Before attempting to have a conversation with someone, develop not a crime theory, but rather a Sales Crime Theory that gives a specific reason why we are contacting this buyer for a conversation right now.

To find that reason, ask yourself the foundation question of a Sales Crime Theory.

Why should they want to talk with you right now?

Many salespeople see this question through a different lens and ask themselves why they should talk with this buyer. One of the goals when prospecting is to gain DI engagement. We are trying to motivate them to explore a relationship with us. Asking yourself why you should talk with them, instead of the other way around, places the focus erroneously on you. The focus, however, should be on what would motivate this person to explore what you have to offer.

Activity Quantity versus Quality

Some see sales as merely a numbers game. They think that if you make enough calls you will be successful in sales. I argue that quantity alone does not assure success. Activity quantity is certainly important, but the quality of each call is also a necessity. Developing a Sales Crime Theory before making calls adds a qualitative element to your prospecting activities.

People no longer tolerate being the sales call of the day, nor do they allow you to come into their offices asking what it is they do, in search of a problem to solve. Their expectation is that before you call them, you've done your homework and have a reason why they should have a conversation with you today.

That may be what buyers expect, but few salespeople do it. It is expected that salespeople will hear countless "no's" before getting a single "yes." That failure is exacerbated by poor sales prospecting strategies. Thus, quantity of calls alone won't get you where you need to be. The quality of each interaction in the buying process ultimately determines your sales fate.

Perils of Voicemail Messages

In today's technological age, salespeople are most likely to get voicemail during most of their prospecting efforts. If you are lucky enough to reach someone on the phone, you need to make the most out of that interaction, which is exactly what a Sales Crime Theory helps you do.

With a Sales Crime Theory developed, you have the information needed to craft a compelling voicemail message. Salespeople often tell me that leaving voicemail messages frustrates them. "No one calls me back!" They look to me for pearls of wisdom to make their phone ring with return calls.

Rather than give an answer, I ask them why that person should call them back.

"What message did you leave to help that person recognize he should want to talk with you now?"

Unless what you have to offer cuts a prospect's costs by an inconceivable amount, the standard voicemail message—leaving your company name, your name, and your phone number—won't lead to a return call.

However, by using Sales Crime Theory evidence, you can craft an effective message that either leads to a return call or prepares a DI for a conversation with you.

Finding Sales Crime Theory Evidence

Imagine you are reading the current issue of your local *Business Journal.* You come across an interview with the CEO at XYZ Manufacturers. During the interview, the CEO shares his initiative for next year, which is to make his company more efficient and reduce costs. The efficiency and cost reduction initiatives provide you with Sales Crime Theory evidence. If *WHAT you sell* addresses those two points, you have what you need to connect the evidence to your solution and formulate a Sales Crime Theory that is communicated in *HOW you sell*.

Putting Together a Sales Crime Theory

Based on the evidence you gather, develop a compelling message, one for the target entry point for the account, based on what you have to offer that helps the person recognize he should want to talk with you right now. For example:

> "Good morning, Mr. Jones. I recently read an interview with your CEO regarding initiatives for the upcoming year, which are to become more efficient and reduce costs. Given your role as the head of manufacturing, I'm sure you play an important role with the success of those two initiatives. Our solutions help manufacturers like you increase efficiency and reduce cost. What is your availability next week for us to meet and discuss how we can help you achieve those two objectives?"

If you didn't develop a Sales Crime Theory, your call would have been based on guesswork.

> "As the head of manufacturing, I'm guessing you are trying to increase efficiency and reduce cost."

You hope you are lucky and make a connection with that expression, but just like with the lottery, you need to be very lucky. You also sound like every other salesperson calling on this person, which means a low likelihood of intriguing him to meet with you.

Rather than leave the connection to chance, put together a Sales Crime Theory that shows genuine interest in the account (shown by the fact you did the homework) and connects the dots for them (you've identified the synergy between their objectives and your solution).

Competitor Evidence

Sales Crime Theory evidence can also be found when analyzing the competitive landscape. Is the incumbent provider having issues with technology, operations, distribution, quality, turnover, financials, or billing? Any of those provides you with Sales Crime Theory evidence such that a DI should want to talk with you now.

If you keep your ear to the ground with your prospects/clients and follow the news, you can readily find evidence relative to your competition. If you hear about multiple quality issues with the same providers, you can use that evidence to further investigate and formulate a Sales Crime Theory. In this case, ask yourself how quality issues affect clients. Who do those issues impact? Why is the quality issue important?

The answers to those questions give you what you need to determine who to contact and what the approach should be to help that person recognize he should want to talk with you now. An approach could be:

> "Good morning, Mr. Jones. I understand you are the head of manufacturing. The reason for my call is that we have had several manufacturing leaders of late contact us for help with improving quality. Given that is a responsibility of yours and that we help manufacturing leaders like you improve quality, perhaps we should have a conversation. What is your availability next week to explore ways we can help you improve quality?"

Notice that I never bashed the competition. I didn't mention them at all. What I did do was plant the seed that his manufacturing colleagues are looking for ways to improve quality and are contacting us for help. I left the door open for him to share if he is having quality issues.

I also helped him visualize the synergy between his goals and what we offer. Rather than push for a meeting, I used words like "perhaps" and "conversation" to come across in a nontraditional salesperson fashion, which is different than what the competition would have done.

Why You Are Contacting Them Now

The Sales Crime Theory gives purpose to your outreach. Sometimes you will share the evidence you found like I did in the first example with the *Business Journal.* In other cases, that information is kept to yourself as I did in the second example.

Here are several examples of Sales Crime Theory evidence:

ABOUT THEM

- They have public relations news.
- They have new locations.
- They have a new product or service launching.
- Their company has a new corporate objective.
- They were acquired.
- They hired a new executive.
- Changes in regulation impact their business.
- There's a new trend—a best practice that can help them.
- There are provider consolidation opportunities that can make them more efficient.
- They are being sued.
- They acquired a company.
- They won an award.
- The have a new initiative or directive.

ABOUT YOU

- You have new locations.
- You are the new salesperson in the territory.
- You were acquired.

- You have clients in the same vertical industry.
- You are offering a new product or service.
- You have a new solution to an old problem.

And here are several ways to find Sales Crime Theory evidence about them:

- Research the prospect company for news and announcements.
- Research their competitors in search of advantages their competitors have over the company you plan to contact. Look for aspects you can help them address.
- Research their industry to learn trends and best practices through their associations.
- Research your industry for upcoming changes to regulation or new best practices.
- Research your competitors for hiring news, acquisition news, and word on the street about performance.
- Research Decision Influencers to find out their concerns and goals. Connect those to the solutions you offer.

> It's easy to find DIs who can say "no." Your challenge is to find the ones who have the authority to say "yes."

Most of this research can be performed online through direct visits to websites and Google searches. Google Alerts are an easy, free way to receive Sales Crime Theory evidence right in your inbox. Search "Google Alerts" in Google and you will find directions to easily set these up. You can monitor your competitors, industries, people, etc. If you aren't using these, you are missing out on a great information source.

Call Those Who Will See Meaningful Value

Salespeople are often frustrated by a constraint that their Decision Influencers have: their budgets. The DI will consider the presented solution relative to his budget and make a decision. Often that decision is to put off the solution until next year when the budget is revisited.

If your solution has a strong business case and your DI is telling you to wait until next year, consider that you may be talking to the wrong level in the account. Something is wrong if *WHAT you sell* provides a strong return on investment and the DI isn't jumping all over it.

> **Don't call on those constrained by budgets, but rather those who can create them.**

It's easy to find DIs who can say "no." Your challenge is to find the ones who have the authority to say "yes."

If you are accustomed to selling to mid-level management and often hit this roadblock, start calling at a higher level in the organization. Someone in the C-Suite wants to hear about a business case solution that can impact the company's financial performance. Research to find "evidence" that demonstrates why those in the C-Suite should want to have a conversation with you now and put together a strategy to engage them. Don't call on those constrained by budgets, but rather those who can create them.

When we look at the *HOW you sell* component of your sales differentiation strategy, the name of the game is to sell differently than the competition. Some salespeople say they are "relationship salespeople." That's their success strategy. When I ask them to define the expression, they usually struggle to do it. Then I ask, "If you don't have a relationship, how do you get in the door as a relationship salesperson?" To that question, I hear total silence in response. All salespeople need a creative way to engage buyers, so they stand out from the competition, which is exactly what the Sales Crime Theory strategy does for you.

This strategy effectively differentiates your prospecting approach and gets you in the door. The research and preparation work you've done prior to reaching out makes for a positive experience for DIs. This paves the way for them to see buying from you is the right choice.

SALES DIFFERENTIATION CONCEPT #11

A Sales Crime Theory differentiates you by answering this question: *Why should this buyer want to talk with you right now?*

CHAPTER 12

THE MOST IMPORTANT SALES DIFFERENTIATION TOOL

Salespeople strive for differentiation, but they have to be careful that the differentiation they create is viewed as they intended. With that in mind, I can't emphasize enough the importance of word selection. There are some expressions that excite buyers and compel them to want to do business with you. There are others that quickly turn buyers off. Care and planning are required so that the words you use differentiate in the way in which you intend. That's why "word selection" is the most important *HOW you sell* sales differentiation tool in a salesperson's toolbox.

We've all been in sales situations, on the buyer side of the table, where we heard a word or phrase that caught our attention. In some cases, it was positive for the sale and in others it was negative. After the salesperson uttered those words, we heard nothing else. Those words played a major role in our buying decision.

Experience Is Meaningless

Two boys, Steven and David, begin playing Little League baseball at the age of eight. When they turn twelve, they are eligible for the Little

League All-Star team. This All-Star program is the one you see on ESPN every July and August, "The Road to Williamsport." Since both boys are twelve years old and they each have five years of experience, which one should be chosen for the All-Star team?

Well? Which one should be selected? What's your hesitation in coming up with your answer?

It seems like some important information is missing. How could someone determine which player is better based on the number of years they've played? "Years" doesn't necessarily translate into skill. It simply means they've played the game for some period of time, not that they are any good at it.

Think about the last meeting you had with a Decision Influencer. I'll bet at some point you shared the number of years your company has been in business. You shared that number expecting to hit a home run with your DI. But don't you think they thought, as you did when you read my "all-star selection" question, that information was missing for that point to be meaningful? You told your DI about your company's years of experience, but it doesn't mean you are any good at what you do.

Just like the baseball example, information is missing when you talk in terms of experience, which is what most salespeople do. They share their years as a strategy to differentiate themselves from the competition with an expectation that DIs will be wowed when they hear "experience." Years of experience is as meaningless in business as it is in baseball because it doesn't speak to your skill mastery.

Expertise Differentiates

Experience only has value if expertise was acquired. DIs want to know about the mastery you've developed—your expertise in helping people just like them achieve their goals. Not only is that what they want to hear, but that message differentiates you from all other salespeople calling on them. Position your expertise in a meaningful way with DIs and it will be music to their ears. Let your competitors preach experience while you position expertise. You can say something such as:

> "We've been in business for fifteen years. During these years, we've encountered every challenge that executives in your role have faced and we've developed solutions to help our clients address these problems."

A statement like that gives context to the years you've been in business. It addresses why such a differentiator should matter to your buyer.

This differentiation of experience and expertise doesn't just hold true for the description of your company, but also for yourself. If you've been talking about the number of years you've spent in an industry (or working for the company), give some thought to the mastery you've developed during that time. Share how your expertise provides value to your clients. That's a great way to differentiate yourself from the competition. You could say something like:

Differentiation of experience and expertise doesn't just hold true for the description of your company, but also for yourself.

> "I've been in this industry for ten years. During this time, I've had the opportunity to help many executives, who have had challenges similar to yours, develop solutions that help them address those."

Just like the company statement, this expression of your years in an industry is presented in a way that positions your expertise, which serves as a meaningful differentiator.

The Power of One Word

In Chapter 10, I shared the story about the technology training company. At that company, we had three sales teams to serve our three core markets: corporate, government, and consumer. The consumer market was focused on career changers. These were people who saw the incredible employment opportunities available in IT but lacked the training to qualify them for those jobs.

Every Sunday, we advertised in the employment section of the *Washington Post* to generate career changer phone leads on Monday. The only acceptable outcome from those inbound calls was scheduled consultations at our facility.

When we looked at our team's appointment-setting conversion rates, we found an intriguing dynamic. It turned out we had two types of salespeople: those who were fantastic at booking appointments and those who were unsuccessful at it. We had no average performers on the team. Given that performance dynamic, we decided to listen to some of the inbound calls to find out why we had this delta.

First, we listened to the calls of salespeople who were effective at scheduling appointments. They reached a point in the conversation where they said, "The way we begin the process with all of our prospective students is with a consultation."

Then we listened to salespeople who struggled to set these appointments. At the same point in the call, they said, "Typically, we have you come in for a consultation."

What was the newly introduced word? "Typically!" And what does "typically" mean? There are other ways this can be handled. When career changers heard "typically," they asked if the salesperson could mail or fax the information to them. As soon as we were able to stop the low-performing salespeople from using that word, their appointment-conversion rates rose and matched the rest of the sales team. One word made all of the difference.

What words and expressions are you using that create unnecessary sales obstacles for you?

Two Words Guaranteed to Turn DIs Off

There are two words that are pervasive in the sales profession and deeply engrained in the English language. We use these words without giving the slightest consideration of how they could be heard by someone else. Commonly used to start sentences, these two words are guaranteed to turn buyers off.

Those two words are: *"I want."*

In sales, these two words are often used in the following ways:

> *"I want to meet with you."*
>
> *"I want to learn about your business."*
>
> *"I want to tell you about our products."*
>
> *"I want to show you a demo of our technology."*
>
> *"I want to meet your colleagues."*

Many sales training courses teach salespeople to begin sales calls with "What I want to do today is . . .". The rationale behind this approach is that it sets an agenda for the meeting. Agenda-setting is a sales best practice, but this word selection communicates to the person with whom you are meeting that you are there for your purposes, not theirs. "I want" creates that unintended perception.

When buyers hear "I want," they immediately think, "Of course. You want to sell me something and get a commission." How can you build a relationship and sell to someone who feels this way about you? You can't.

Rule of thumb: There is only one person in the world, other than you, who cares what you want. It's Mom! No one else cares what you want.

You've probably noticed a continued reference in this book to "win more deals at the prices you want." Buyers obviously don't care to help you protect margin. They want the cheapest price they can get, which makes you taking ownership of winning deals at desired price points critical to the health of your company.

When communicating with DIs, your goal is to be perceived as different—in a positive way. The way that you can be different in *HOW you sell* is to put their interests in the forefront. The way that you do that is through word selection, so perception and reality are one and the same.

What DIs want to know is:

> *Why should I meet with you?*
>
> *Why should I tell you about my business?*
>
> *Why should I learn about your products?*
>
> *Why should I see a demo of your technology?*
>
> *Why should I introduce you to my colleagues?*

I frequently receive requests from salespeople asking for sales guidance. One of the most common is for help with "stuck deals."

"How do I get buyers to introduce me to others in their company?" they ask.

My response—a question, not a statement—always surprises them.

"Why should they introduce you to their colleagues?"

If they can't come up with an answer, they know why they've been unable to expand account relationships.

Because "I want" is so deeply a part of our communication style, shifting to this new way of communicating doesn't come naturally for all salespeople. Before having a conversation with a DI, introspectively consider what the benefit would be for her to meet with you, to tell you about her business, to learn about your products, to see your technology, and to introduce you to her colleagues. You need answers to those questions to be different from all of the other salespeople calling on this account and to take steps toward building relationships.

Beware of Industry Jargon

Not only do you need to be mindful of the words you use, but also how you hear the words they share with you. A great example of this is in the health club industry. A health club member inquires about "personal training." The response he hears is that the service costs $100 per hour. He walks away frustrated. Why is he frustrated? The question he was actually asking was, "Can someone help me get started with a program and show me how to use the equipment?" This service is usually offered for free.

Because "personal training" services has an industry definition associated with it, health club workers unknowingly frustrate their members. They refer to this as a "new member orientation," but only people within the industry would ever use that expression. The public describes it in terms they know: "personal training." Think about the jargon pervasive in your industry. Does it cause communication disconnects between you and your buyers?

Another example is a buyer's request for a "demo" or presentation. Most salespeople hear those requests and turn into lecturers. Handling those requests as one-directional communication events are a surefire way to lose the deal. Let your competitors fall prey to that trap. Make those events conversational—even in large groups. Even though they used the words "demo" and presentation, DIs still desire two-way communication, not a lecture.

Exciting Your Decision Influencers

Earlier in the chapter, I shared two words that turn DIs off, but there is also one word that excites them. Most salespeople don't use this word enough. It's a word that can differentiate *HOW you sell*. It's the word "help." Help is viewed positively by most DIs. After all, who wouldn't want help to improve effectiveness, drive profitability, increase revenue, defeat competitors, improve productivity, and enhance efficiency?

Notice that I said that most people view the word "help" positively. There are some people who might see the word as an insult because there hasn't been agreement on aspects that need outside assistance. An example:

> "We help customer service managers improve the effectiveness of their teams."

If the customer service manager has not already acknowledged a performance issue, "help" could be perceived negatively. Again, this speaks to the care of word selection.

No More Customers!

How you describe business relationships can also differentiate *HOW you sell*. Most business people describe those who buy from them as "customers." If you look up the word "customer" in the dictionary, you find that it simply means "one who buys from another." There is no deeper meaning to it. The word "customer" simplifies the relationship between you and your buyers. It's nothing more than someone buying stuff from you. I have yet to encounter a salesperson who intends to communicate that message.

On the other side, these so-called "customers" use a word that drives salespeople batty. It's the word "vendor." Salespeople hate when they are referred to in that way because it means no value is perceived in the relationship as described by the DI.

In Spanish, the word *vender* means "to sell." The word "vendor" simplifies the relationship between buyer and seller. It's nothing more than someone selling you stuff.

Putting this together, a customer buys from a vendor. Neither party appreciates being referred to in these terms.

You will never hear a lawyer or accountant say they have a customer. They have clients. If you look up the word "client" in the dictionary, it says "one who is under the protection of another." The relationship has a value beyond a monetary exchange. Think about the solutions you offer. Are you offering protection to those with whom you have business relationships? If so, consider that you have clients, not customers.

For the sales team that I managed in the employment screening industry, we recognized this as an opportunity to differentiate *HOW you sell*. Our salespeople told buyers "we have no customers," which shocked them. They would ask, "How do you have no customers and still pay the bills?" We would then explain that we don't have customers, but we do have clients—and lots of them. Perhaps, you can differentiate yourself this way as well.

"We recognize the importance of what we provide, the impact we have on your business, and appreciate the trust our clients place in us."

While the concept of word selection as a sales differentiation strategy may seem subtle, it's not. The right word or wrong word can be the difference between winning the deal at the prices you want . . . or not. Notice I referenced not just winning deals, but also protecting price points through word selection.

When I managed sales teams, my top salespeople rehearsed with me when preparing for critical DI conversations. I didn't require them to do that, but they recognized that there was often no margin for error in those conversations. They saw the importance of differentiating *HOW you sell* through word selection.

SALES DIFFERENTIATION CONCEPT #12

The words salespeople use, and do not use, differentiate them.

CHAPTER 13

THE ART OF QUERY TO POSITION DIFFERENTIATORS

When I was very young, adults often told me that I should pursue a career in sales. I heard it again in high school, again in college and, yet again, post-graduation. Perhaps people told you that you too had what it took to be a great salesperson.

Why did people encourage us to pursue a sales career? There was one reason. We were great talkers! People not in the sales profession think that "talking" is the key to sales success. Certainly, being articulate is an ingredient in the sales success recipe, but that is not the one that makes someone a sales rock star.

Those of us in the sales profession know that what you say to a Decision Influencer is not the secret to winning in sales. Many people in this profession think the number one sales success factor is listening. I constantly hear sales managers preaching the importance of listening skills to their salespeople. Listening is also an ingredient in the sales success recipe, but there is still one skill that is even more important to master.

They Don't Know How to Buy

A foundation element of your sales differentiation strategy is the recognition that you know more about the world of potential solutions in your industry than your buyers do. While salespeople agree with me on that point, they quickly forget it when they see business cards with titles like CFO, COO, president, and CEO. Those titles dupe salespeople into believing buyers know at least as much they as do about the world of solutions. But buyers don't.

> A foundation element of your sales differentiation strategy is the recognition that you know more about the world of potential solutions in your industry than your buyers do.

Not only do those executives not know as much as you about the solutions, most of them don't know how to make the right purchasing decision for those solutions. They have a specialized expertise in their respective roles, but not in every product, service, and technology they procure. This creates an opportunity for salespeople to help them make the right decisions.

While the executives may not have the expertise that you do with respect to your industry solutions, if your approach is "telling," you're in for a very short meeting. No one wants to be lectured, not even children. What you are saying may be completely accurate, but the message falls on deaf ears because of how it is communicated.

"Listening" won't get you shown the door, but if DIs don't know all the solutions available (improved performance, cost reduction, provider reduction, etc.), what will you listen for? If they don't know that an alternative solution can potentially better fit their needs, they can't possibly articulate it.

Top salespeople and sales managers recognize that the number one, most critical skill leading to sales success is the art of query—asking DIs questions that help them think differently about the solutions they have or could have. Listening is important, but the right questions need to be asked so there is pertinent information to be heard. The information shared by the DI is the information that helps a salesperson to construct a sale—to build a solution. The art of query creates an opportunity in *HOW you sell* to provide meaningful value.

I've found that when it comes to pre-call planning, most salespeople focus their time on what they will say to a buyer. "I'm going to tell them about this product or service." Few plan the questions they can ask to differentiate themselves during the sales call.

What to Ask

During an initial sales call, a buyer could be asked an infinite number of questions. However, you have a finite amount of time for the meeting and there are only so many questions you can ask before the DI feels like she is the target of an interrogation. That's certainly not helpful in your selling effort. That means every question must be well-planned because every minute of face time you get with a buyer is precious. Given the universe of potential questions, how do you decide which ones to ask?

Setting the Destination

Imagine you are planning a trip. The first question to be answered is the destination. Without knowing where you are going, you can't develop a plan to get there. The same holds true for architecting an effective sales call. You need to know the destination, the criteria for success, to be able to put together a plan achieve it.

I often ask senior executives about their sales teams relative to initial buyer meetings.

> *"If all your salespeople called you after an initial DI meeting and told you they just had a great meeting, what do you know for certain happened during that meeting?"*

Most of them stumble in their responses and say they couldn't answer that question universally for their sales force. Each of their salespeople has a different approach to the handling of sales calls for the same type of buyer. No wonder companies struggle to understand their sales forecasts!

Consider *HOW you sell* sales differentiation when it comes to handling an initial meeting with a buyer. What can you do differently than your competitors in that meeting that would cause a DI to feel she received meaningful value? Rather than ask arbitrary questions, put together a focused plan that provides value for both your buyer and you.

Coming back to my point about defining the destination first, ask yourself:

It was a great first meeting if I accomplished what?

In many B2B sales, getting the order is not a likely expectation as a result of an initial meeting, so success has to be defined in other terms. In other words, we need to identify the desired outcomes we seek from the first meeting. Here is a list of potential outcomes for consideration in your "great first meeting portfolio" (presented in no particular order).

For this to have been a great first meeting, you learned:

- Who would be involved in making the decision
- Their timeframe to make a decision
- Why they are looking to make a change
- The criteria for making a change in provider
- How they buy
- Their budget
- The current providers and others under consideration
- The solution provided by the current providers
- Their satisfaction level with the current providers—what they like and dislike
- What they are presently paying their current providers

- The payment terms with their current provider
- The renewal provisions in their provider's contract
- Their corporate goals and how you fit within them
- Their personal goals and how you fit within them
- Why they accepted a meeting with you

For this to have been a great first meeting, you demonstrated:

- Expertise in your industry
- Expertise in the solutions you offer
- Expertise in their industry

For this to have been a great first meeting, you also:

- Scheduled another meeting
- Scheduled a demo
- Set defined action steps with a timeline
- Received a referral to other parts of the company
- Were introduced to others involved in making the decision
- Received a referral to other companies
- Toured their facility
- Qualified the opportunity for size and scope to determine if this is the right fit for your company
- Gained interest in exploring a relationship with your company
- Established trust and took the first steps toward building a relationship
- Positioned relevant differentiators in *WHAT you sell* and those differentiators matter to them
- Differentiated yourself and provided meaningful value through *HOW you sell*

Of course, not all these potential outcomes belong on your list, but many of them do. Your first step, when strategizing to differentiate yourself during a sales call, is to develop the criteria for a great first meeting. The list I provided gets you started down that path. Once you've identified the outcomes, you've set your destination. Those outcomes allow you to create a roadmap for your meeting which is defined by asking:

What am I going to ask, say, and do to achieve each of the identified outcomes?

Question Types

A plan is needed to achieve each of the outcomes you seek from the initial DI meeting. The first step is to identify the questions to be asked. From the infinite portfolio of questions that potentially could be posed, select only ones that help you achieve the desired outcomes.

Some questions are what I call *data collection*. They are factual in nature:

- How many locations do you have?
- Who manages the program?
- What are your department's goals for the year?

Another type of question is a *challenge question*. These are questions that expose aspects that a buyer perceives can be better or different from what she already has. Some examples of challenge questions are:

- If there were one area of the program that could be better, what would it be?
- What are some of the challenges you've had with the program?
- If you could create the ideal solution for your needs, what would it include?

- What are three things you would like to have that you don't have today?

Challenge questions help you assess aspects a buyer perceives could be better or different. However, buyers don't know what you know. They aren't aware of the enhancements they could have, but don't. If you ask challenge questions exclusively, there's a high probability of the status quo winning the deal because the buyer does not perceive a challenge or an area that could be improved.

> Challenge questions help you assess aspects a buyer perceives could be better or different.

Plus, challenge questions don't help a buyer to think differently about a potential solution because these questions are limited to the buyer's perceptions. This necessitates another type of query—a *positioning question*—to differentiate *HOW you sell*.

Positioning questions are open-ended (not yes or no) and align with your differentiators. These questions help buyers think differently about the solutions they have or could have.

Unlike challenge questions, positioning questions expose areas that a buyer does *not* perceive could be better or different. Buyers consider the product or service they presently have and accept performance as industry standard. They do not voice dissatisfaction with it. What if you possess differentiators that can disrupt their status quo perception and provide improved performance? How can you lead DIs to see that opportunity?

> Unlike challenge questions, positioning questions expose areas that a buyer does *not* perceive could be better or different.

For example, what if you have the differentiated ability to improve speed, increase quality, or reduce costs, creating a superior solution to what they have today? Challenge questions will not bring that conversation to the forefront because the buyers don't know it could be better or different. Lecturing them on the alternative solution, without first gaining interest in having the conversation, fails to engage them. Positioning questions open the door with buyers by arousing interest in alternative solutions.

Wipe Differently

Imagine you are selling a product that attempts to disrupt a centuries-old market. That's what Ryan Meegan is attempting to do with Dude Wipes. He was interviewed by *Men's Health* magazine about his flushable wipes product—an alternative to toilet paper. This solution is much more expensive than dry paper, and people are accustomed to a way of handling their wiping needs. So, to lead people to consider his product, he needs to help them think differently about the solution.

"If you were to get chocolate on your arm or hand, you would not just use a dry paper towel and call it a day, right?" Meegan says in the article. "You'd use a wet paper towel or a wipe to make sure you got all of the substance."

He could also turn this into a positioning question:

"If you got chocolate on your arm, how would you clean it off?"

That certainly leads a buyer to think differently! Gross example, perhaps, but it's an effective metaphor to help buyers think differently about a solution they've probably never thought about. If he can't disrupt buyer complacency, no one will consider this wiping alternative.

Lock Up the Deal!

Would you pay ninety-nine dollars for a padlock? Most of us wouldn't consider spending that much on a lock. Yet, that's what Tapplock is suggesting we do. Like Dude Wipes, they are trying to disrupt buyer complacency with a new solution to an old problem.

They offer differentiators comparing their padlock to traditional pad-locks. One of those differentiators is that Tapplock offers three ways to unlock the device: fingerprint, Bluetooth, and phone. I've never spoken with them, but I thought about the way I would disrupt buyer compla-cency surrounding this product with positioning questions.

"When you've lost the combination for your padlock (because we all have), what did you do with the lock?"

Another positioning question I would ask is:

"When your padlock gets rusty, what do you do with it?"

Most people, in response to both questions, will say they toss the lock in the trash. This product offers a durable lock with a way to ensure "forever" use.

Trashy Question

In an earlier chapter, I shared the story of my client in the waste disposal industry. This company offers a service that no other garbage hauler in the state of Minnesota offers. Twice per year, they clean a homeowner's garbage cans free of charge. Again, no other hauler in Minnesota offers this service to their clients—even for a fee.

Given the fact that no one else offers this service, a challenge question inquiring about desired service enhancements will not help move the sale forward. On his own, will a homeowner say he would appreciate having a trash company that cleans his garbage cans? That's not likely to happen because he doesn't know this service exists.

For their residential salespeople, we developed a positioning ques-tion for this innovative service that is to be asked at the beginning of the sales call:

"When is the last time you had your garbage cans cleaned?"

They ask this positioning question because the only way a homeowner's garbage cans have been cleaned is if he did it himself. Most likely, he has never had them cleaned and his garage stinks because of trash residue.

By asking this question early in the conversation, right in the first few moments of a sales interaction, those salespeople have helped a buyer to think differently about something as basic as trash service. The buyer thinks differently not because of something the salesperson said, but rather because of a question that was asked.

Leading Buyers to See the Solution

If you've ever been in a courtroom or you watch court television, you know that attorneys can't testify. They can only ask questions of witnesses. Those questions are crafted to paint the picture for the decision makers—the jury—that the attorney wants them to see. That's what positioning questions do for you. They help you paint a picture for Decision Influencers through query, not lecture.

If you've ever been under the care of a psychiatrist or psychologist, you know they don't give you the answers. They ask questions leading you down a path, so you see what they see. Positioning questions do that for you as well. They help buyers recognize the issue and the need to address it without you having to tell them to do it. To disrupt complacency, questions need to be asked that help them to think differently about the solutions they have or could have. I often refer to positioning questions as status quo disrupters.

Coming back to the concept of differentiating through *HOW you sell*, handing sales calls in this way is an experience most buyers have never had. They come away feeling educated, but not insulted. After all, you have informed through questioning rather than lecturing.

Developing Positioning Questions

Here is how to create your positioning questions. For each of the differentiators you identified through the exercises in Chapter 5, go through these five steps:

1. **Relevancy.** Ask yourself why a specific differentiator matters to a Decision Influencer. Some examples are cost savings, efficiency, improvement, and compliance. If you can't answer this question, consider that, while this may be a differentiator, it is not one that helps you win deals at the prices you want.

2. **Decision Influencers.** As addressed in Chapter 6, not all differentiators matter to all DIs. Given that, identify the individuals with whom this differentiator is most likely to resonate. For example, if it has financial ramifications, it would matter to those with fiduciary responsibilities like business owners and CFOs.

3. **Symptoms.** Under what circumstances does this differentiator matter to a DI? You may learn this information during your pre-call research. You may also learn this during the conversation with a buyer or you may observe it. For example, if the differentiator helps improve workplace safety and you learned that they've had a significant number of on-the-job injuries, that symptom alerts you that this differentiator should strike a chord with this buyer. Your research for Sales Crime Theory evidence helps align symptoms with DI priorities.

4. **Positioning Questions.** Based on steps one through three, craft an open-ended question that exposes the relevancy of the differentiator for the identified DIs. You may need to create multiple positioning questions for a differentiator, given the identified DIs and symptoms. Your positioning questions should be designed to help someone think differently about the solution they have or could have (such as the wipes, locks, and garbage can cleaning service). Positioning questions

are always open-ended, because otherwise a short answer of *no* slams the door shut for a conversation about the differentiator.

5. **Discussion.** Once the positioning questions have opened the door and the DI is receptive to learning about this aspect, identify the information to be shared relative to the differentiator. This can be in the form of statistics, factual information, case studies, and client examples.

Coming back to the reverse engineering of a sales call exercise, we've addressed how to develop the outcomes portfolio and the questions to be asked. What you will "say" and "do" during the meeting is, similar to the questions you will "ask," a function of the outcomes that you seek.

Asking the right questions, in the right fashion, creates intrigue about what your company has to offer. However, the key is to make sure that questions aren't posed in such a way that they create the feeling of an interrogation. Use of what I refer to as "insulators" helps soften your questions and keeps the meeting conversational. They are used as buffers both before and /or after asking questions.

Examples of insulators as introductions to questions:

- I don't know if this would make sense for you . . .
- Just out of curiosity . . .
- I'm not quite sure how to phrase this . . .

Examples of insulators shared after asking questions:

- . . . The reason I asked was . . .
- . . . Which is why I was asking
- . . . Not to put you on the spot
- . . . But this may not make sense for you

As the initial meeting with a DI concludes, how do you know if your sales differentiation strategy was effective? As you end the meeting, ask your buyer one final question:

"What did we talk about today that was different from what you expected we would talk about?"

The answer to that question tells you the value he received from the meeting and provides foundational insight for future ones.

SALES DIFFERENTIATION CONCEPT #13

It's not what salespeople *say* to buyers, but rather what they *ask* of buyers, that differentiates them from the competition.

CHAPTER 14

SHAPING BUYER DECISION CRITERIA

I n Chapter 5, when I talked about the purchase of organic apples, I said that the buyer bought the more expensive organic apple because "organic" was important to her as a consumer. The decision wasn't driven by anything the salesperson said or did. The buyer set the criteria for what she wanted to buy.

Truth be told, I've never purchased an organic apple. It's not because I'm opposed to organic, but rather because I don't know why it matters. There is a lot of marketing around the expression "organic" and buyers define that value in many ways.

In my search for "organic value," I found several articles on the subject. The main argument in all of them is that organic apples have no pesticides sprayed on them. The selling point is that there are medical concerns associated with pesticides.

Aside from taste, most of us are uneducated consumers when it comes to purchasing apples. Price certainly affects our decision-making. In August 2017, the national average price of organic apples was $2.34 per pound while non-organic apples were $1.57 per pound. Thus, organic apples are almost 50 percent more expensive than non-organic apples. That's a significant price difference that likely impacts a buyer's decision-making.

Setting Decision Criteria

Suppose you sell both organic and non-organic apples. When a consumer arrives in your store, would you take the time to position the meaningful differences between the organic and non-organic apples? Most salespeople would not. They leave the setting of decision-making criteria to the consumers. After all, buyers know what they want. Or do they?

Returning to an earlier point, most consumers don't know the difference between the two apples. I asked twenty randomly selected people what the difference is between organic and non-organic apples, and only two knew the correct answer. Granted that's a small sample, but I'm guessing the percentages wouldn't change much in a larger sample.

Given that such a small percentage of people know the difference between them, the majority will look at the apples as two pieces of fruit, one of which costs almost 50 percent more than the other. Which one do you think most people will buy? Of course, most will pick the lower-priced apple.

This apple byte parallels a flawed belief held by many salespeople. They assume that DIs know how to buy what they sell. They erroneously allow these people to set decision-making criteria which leads many to make the wrong decision for their needs. Most buyers don't know the criteria to buy an apple. Do you think they know how to buy what you sell?

I've posed the following question to thousands of salespeople over the years:

> *"Who knows more about the world of possible solutions your industry has to offer . . . you or your buyers?"*

So far, no salespeople have said that the people they sell to have a greater knowledge about the world of possible solutions than they do. If that's the case, how come salespeople leave the determination of decision criteria to their buyers? Do you see both a problem and an opportunity? Salespeople have an opportunity to shape buyer decision criteria, but many miss out on it, leading to flawed decision-making by their DIs.

The organic apple salespeople could have helped shape buyer decision criteria and provided meaningful value in *HOW you sell*. They could have asked questions and shared information to educate buyers, leading them to see the meaningful, differentiated value of organic fruit. People don't know how to buy *WHAT you sell*, and you can find examples of this everywhere.

> People don't know how to buy *WHAT you sell*, and you can find examples of this everywhere.

Cold Light

The lighting industry is undergoing a major shift to LED bulbs. These bulbs have a great return on investment as they use 90 percent less energy than standard incandescent bulbs, according to CBS Denver. Energy reduction for lighting is one of the LED bulb differentiators. Another differentiator is that these bulbs emit significantly less heat.

The city of Denver, Colorado converted their traffic lights to LED bulbs. What they may not have considered was a critical function that their former light bulb solution provided: heat.

Denver gets a lot of snow. Some of it accumulates on traffic lights, which creates a driving hazard. The standard incandescent bulbs produced enough heat to melt it, but LED bulbs do not. Drivers' inability to see the traffic lights has led to accidents. Now Denver will have to do something about its hazardous traffic lights. The LED change may have seemed like a no-brainer at the time, but it was also a missed opportunity for a salesperson to educate the buyer on the ramifications of the decision. Buyers need your help!

Tree Hugging

In June 2016, a massive storm came through the Minneapolis suburb in which I live. It was a storm different than any I've ever experienced. It wasn't classified as a tornado because it had straight winds in excess of eighty miles per hour. If the winds had been in the shape of a funnel, the storm would have been designated an F1 tornado.

While the storm turned day into night, I was still able to see the huge trees in my backyard break and tumble like toys. The next morning, I looked at my yard and saw the disaster. Large limbs had fallen on my fence and turned it into scrap metal. Some of the trees that came down were so big that if you bear-hugged them, your hands would not meet. In addition to the downed trees, several standing trees were badly damaged and on the verge of falling.

This wasn't the kind of mess where you call on your neighbors with chainsaws for cleanup help. Plus, as my wife loves to remind me, I'm not handy, which meant I needed to hire a contractor (another "guy") to handle it. I had never purchased this type of service before and had no idea how to select a tree service contractor. After notifying my insurance company of the damage, I searched online and found three tree companies to solicit bids for this cleanup project.

The first contractor arrived at my home and took a cursory look at the mess. His quote for the cleanup was $5,000. Since it was the first bid, I didn't know if that was a good price or not.

A representative from the second contractor arrived shortly after the first one left and wandered my yard for an hour shaking his head. He kept muttering to himself, "This is a big job. This is a big job." I almost fell over when he presented his bid. He wanted $12,500—two and a half times the price of the first contractor—to perform the same work. Perhaps, he misunderstood the scope of the project and thought I was asking him to build a log cabin out of the downed trees.

The third contractor's representative walked the yard for a few minutes and said he could have the trees cleaned up for $3,000 dollars. Given the second company's quote, I was shocked by his price, so I asked questions to make sure he wasn't playing games. Was he bidding this project the same way as the other contractors? It turned out he was!

Given the three bids, which company did I hire? I contracted with the third one. Why? None of these companies did anything to differentiate themselves from the others. They all looked at the pile of trees and branches and gave me their price.

They didn't raise any important consideration points when selecting a service provider for the job. The contractors just tossed out a price and hoped to get the work. They didn't ask me any questions that would guide my decision-making. These three companies never tried to differentiate themselves from the pack, even in *HOW you sell*, and let their prices serve as the sole decision factor. I had no other information on which to base my decision.

Coming back to what I shared earlier, I had never purchased this type of service before. I didn't know what to ask of the contractors to make the right decision. What if the expensive provider was the only one with the appropriate insurance for this type of work? That would have affected my decision.

After the job was completed, I learned a few things about downed trees. For example, when a tree falls (rather than breaks), cutting it with a chainsaw causes the bottom portion to snap up at the speed of a rocket. The force created could be deadly! Expertise certainly matters when delivering this type of service, and none of them demonstrated to me that they had it.

Not only were there downed trees, but there were several damaged ones as well. Given that both my neighbors and I have kids and dogs, care was needed when taking down those trees. Again, expertise was required, and I wished one of the contractors had demonstrated it. I picked the cheapest option and hoped for the best.

A point you may have glossed over when reading this story was that I notified my insurance company immediately after the storm. When the trees destroyed my fence, my homeowner's insurance policy became the funding source for the cleanup. Thus, I wasn't paying for the tree cleanup, which meant I didn't care about price. The money wasn't coming out of my pocket; all three of those contractors had the same opportunity to win this deal. All any one of them had to do was differentiate themselves and he would have won the job.

I would also have appreciated counsel on the best way to handle the cleanup and guidance on decision-making criteria that would have differentiated them. As I said, I didn't know what questions to ask the service providers. All I knew was that I had a mess that needed to be cleaned up quickly. Had any of them put their arm around me, walked the yard, and shared the important considerations when doing this type of work, I would have bought from them because they provided meaningful value in *HOW you sell*.

Just like the organic apple example, these salespeople failed to shape decision criteria and help me make the right decision. They missed out on an opportunity to differentiate themselves.

Are you doing the same thing with your buyers that these contractors did with me? Are you leaving them to make a decision based only on price—and becoming angry when they buy from a salesperson with a lower price than yours? If so, I encourage you to revisit *HOW you sell* and identify ways to be meaningfully different from your competition.

Fenced In

There's another story about the fence that was destroyed in the storm. When we first moved into our home, we asked our neighbors for a fence company recommendation. A very nice salesman from the fence company came to visit with my wife and me to talk about the fences his company offered. He showed us an attractive fence and we bought it. Normally, I would shop for something like this, but I needed to get a fence quickly because we had two dogs. Since our neighbors referred the company, we felt comfortable buying without investigating other options.

Several months after the fence was installed, we discovered two issues with the fence that we wished we had known about before we bought it. We planned to have a commercial service handle our lawnmowing, but the gates were too narrow for their mowers to fit through it. How did the salesman not ask me about my lawnmowing plans?

Second, the fence was made of thin aluminum. While it looked great, it bent easily. How did we find that out? Our boys crashed into it a few times while they were playing in the yard. They didn't get hurt, but the fence did. The salesman saw we had young children. Why didn't he recommend a sturdier fence?

At no time did we tell the fence salesman that price was an issue or that we had a set budget for it, so there was no reason to sell us a cheap quality fence or standard gates. I had not bought a fence before, so I didn't know what to ask him. He may have won the deal, but I'm sure he wasn't happy after the conversation I had with the owner of the fence company. While the salesperson was a nice man, he did his company—and more important, me—a disservice.

This highlights the importance of the role salespeople play for buyers. Salespeople need to guide buyer decision-making, so buyers can make informed, educated decisions.

Muddy Decisions

I wish I could say that these situations are the exception, but I find them to be the sales norm. I needed to hire a contractor for mudjacking, which I had never heard of until my neighbors told me about it. Mudjacking is a process used when segments of a concrete driveway become uneven. The service injects mud or sand under the concrete slab to raise it, which restores the uniformity of a driveway or walkway.

For my mudjacking needs, I did the same thing I did for the tree cleanup: solicited three bids and received prices ranging from $600 to $2,000 to complete the job. None of them did anything other than leave a bid sheet in my mailbox. They all missed out on the opportunity to shape my decision criteria and differentiate in *HOW you sell*, so I hired the cheapest one. To this day, I still don't know if there was a difference among them except price.

Most salespeople think that winning deals at the prices you want is challenging. These stories highlight what many of them don't realize, which is how close they really are to winning deals that they lose. The differences in *WHAT you sell* may not be as significant as what you want. However, these deals are being lost to lower prices because salespeople didn't create meaningful value in *HOW you sell*.

Defeating a Beloved Mouse

In my work with clients on sales differentiation, I constantly hear war stories about them trying to knock out the competition. Executives share their frustrations about losing deals and shrinking margins. They talk about the competition as if they are fighting a mythical being, forgetting that even the powerful Achilles had a weakness that led to his downfall. You have an opportunity to take advantage of your competitors' vulnerability through the use of sales differentiation.

If you think your competition is tough, imagine going up against one of the strongest brands in America. This is a brand that is loved by all. When families think of taking a vacation, this is the first brand that comes to mind. Of course, you know I'm referring to Disney.

There's an old expression in B2B sales. "No one ever got fired for buying IBM." IBM had built such a strong brand reputation that their products became known as the safe choice for corporate buyers. Disney enjoys that same quality reputation in the family vacation industry. Picking Disney for a family vacation guarantees a fantastic experience.

Imagine you are selling for Universal Studios and competing against Disney. Their theme parks are near yours. You're both selling family vacations, but you're trying to get people to vacation at your parks instead of Disney's. If you leave setting decision-making criteria to the ones buying vacations, you are probably going to lose. What could Universal Studios do to turn the tide?

During the baseball season, my teenage sons and I often watch the Yankees game on television to wrap up our day. During one game, in between innings, a commercial for Universal Studio's theme park appeared on the screen. Normally, we don't pay attention to commercials during games, but this one captivated us because of something we heard. "Kids grow up, so do vacations."

That expression silenced the room for a moment as we looked at one another. It then led to a fifteen-minute conversation about our vacations. My three kids (I have a daughter, too) range between fifteen and nineteen years old. We've been to Disney World several times and had great experiences. I remember the first time we went there when my daughter was about five years old. She looked at the princesses as if they had jumped off the movie screen. It was amazing to experience Disney through her young eyes.

Yet, Disney World isn't the same magical experience for teenagers as it is for five-year-olds. Universal Studios recognized that too. They launched a differentiation campaign intended to help families think differently about their vacations and shape their decision criteria. Rather than trying to reach families with very young children, they are pursuing those with teenagers. They are fighting for the deals that they can win rather than trying to sell everyone.

Universal Studios is attempting to disrupt conventional thinking of a family vacation (Disney, "the safe family vacation" choice) and have people take a closer look at what they have to offer in their theme parks. They are doing that by shaping decision-making criteria with the consideration of a child's age, giving them a differentiated advantage.

Think about your approach when selling. Do you help your buyers develop criteria or are you leaving that decision to them and taking orders? As one of my clients says, "There's the business that happens to you and the business that you make happen." Never forget that you have a greater knowledge of the possible solutions than they do. Helping shape their decision criteria demonstrates expertise and gives them confidence in you and your company. This component of *HOW you sell* could be the differentiating factor that leads you to win more deals at the prices you want.

SALES DIFFERENTIATION CONCEPT #14

Sales differentiation affords you the opportunity to shape buyer decision criteria.

CHAPTER 15

DISRUPTING THE BUYING PROCESS THROUGH SALES DIFFERENTIATION

People often ask me how a guy from the East Coast wound up living in Minnesota. In short, an employment background screening company recruited me to build a drug testing division for them.

This company's interest in me stemmed from a trend in the employment screening industry. In the early 2000s, buyers of both background screening and drug testing services wanted to procure them from a single source. Until this point, buyers contracted with multiple providers for those services. The market had evolved, and demand was for a consolidated solution for both services. Some, like the company that purchased my former employer, went the acquisition route. Others decided to build it from scratch. That was the strategy my new employer pursued to meet market demand.

Building a Differentiated Solution

For most of my career, I served in sales and marketing leadership capacities. The role with this Minnesota-based firm was much broader and that is what intrigued me about it. My task was to build a workplace drug testing division to complement their employment background screening services. Responsible for sales, marketing, product, operations, pricing, and IT, I was given the keys to the kingdom and asked to deliver results.

The scope of the role and the opportunity to build a differentiated solution had me fired up! Initially, the plan was for me to commute to Minnesota weekly from the Washington, D.C. Metro area, where I was living at the time. However, I quickly realized that this model wouldn't work for my employer or me. To achieve the results I planned to deliver, I needed to relocate to Minnesota and the CEO agreed.

In my prior role, I had heard firsthand from clients what they loved and hated about services in the workplace drug testing industry. They told me what they wanted to be able to accomplish online and described the service model they desired from a third-party administrator (TPA).

Clients also shared their TPA pricing frustrations. They weren't complaining about how much they were paying, but rather that TPAs were secretive about cost information. TPAs commonly provided a fixed price for a drug test. That price comprised the cost of specimen collection, laboratory testing, review of the test by a specially trained and certified doctor (called a medical review officer), and the TPA's services. TPAs did not disclose the costs of the components that rolled up into a price with their clients. That secrecy made clients skeptical about TPA business practices.

On my first day with the Minnesota firm, we got right to work. A team of IT developers greeted me and asked what needed to be built online. We spent several weeks scoping technology that the industry had never seen before. I worked with our operations team to design our services model to align with what the market desired, but that no other TPA offered in that way. We created a differentiated way to handle pricing. The "open book" pricing we offered to clients disclosed all the costs that comprised our price and showed a line-item fee for our services. We took the mysticism and client mistrust out of TPA pricing.

Going for the Big Fish

Right out of the gate, we received great feedback on our business model. The marketplace loved our technology, thought our service model was right on the mark, and found our "open book" pricing refreshing. After several months of winning large deals at the prices we wanted, we decided to pursue the one account that was considered the brass ring of the workplace drug testing industry.

Every TPA wanted this prestigious account in their portfolio because it was a multi-million dollar per year opportunity with very complex requirements. If you could delight this account, others would line up at your door. Having this client in our portfolio would give us instant marketplace credibility. It would mean we were a player.

At the time that we pursued this account, we were no more than a gnat in the industry. We were not on anyone's radar screen as a TPA to watch. No one saw us as a threat. Perhaps they should have.

Over about a year, we had several meetings with the workplace drug testing program manager for this account. He loved our online technology, service model, and pricing methodology. He believed we were the right solution for his firm.

The Three-Letter Acronym All Salespeople Dread

Everything was moving along as planned until late one Friday afternoon when I received a call from the company's program manager. "Lee, I've been doing some checking and found out that, given the amount of money involved, we must go through a formal Request for Proposal (RFP) process to change providers." Hearing that a buyer is going to use an RFP process is the worst news a salesperson can hear. It means there is about to be an attempt to commoditize you.

Not only did the RFP process mean that the selection decision would be delayed, but it also meant procurement officers would be involved in the process. As most salespeople know, the role of procurement is often to commoditize providers and squeeze them on pricing. Many of them devise a matrix to compare providers with the fundamental goal of buying the cheapest solution for their requirements. (Remember Chapter 3 on how people buy.) However, what procurement describes as "the solution" and what their internal client describes as "the solution" usually differ.

While I was disappointed by this turn of events, I asked the program manager to send me the RFP when it was ready. A few weeks later, it arrived in my mailbox. I quickly opened the envelope and began reading the massive document. My jaw hit the floor as I read the scope of the opportunity, which bore no resemblance whatsoever to the yearlong conversations I'd had with the program manager. It was as if the RFP was for some other company. It was obvious that the procurement group had not gathered requirements from the program manager and did not possess the expertise to lead the selection process for their next drug testing TPA.

My team also reviewed the RFP and we met to discuss the scope presented in it. Not only was the scope completely different from our discussions with the program manager, but also the document was structured in a way that made it impossible for us to differentiate ourselves. The document offered no opportunity to position the aspects of our offering that their program manager loved. There was no place to describe our technology, service model, and pricing approach in the RFP. Our *WHAT you sell* differentiators could not be presented in this document.

We also estimated that it would take about a hundred team member hours to respond to the RFP—and we still would be unable to differentiate ourselves. Taking all of this into consideration, we decided to walk away from the account and not respond to their RFP despite the productive meetings we'd had with them. We knew there was no way we would win the deal at the price we wanted, given the way in which they were handling the selection process.

Letting the Big Fish Off the Hook

Since I was the head of the division, I was the one who had to call the program manager and inform him of our decision. Shock is the only word I can use to describe his reaction to my news. I thought he was going to cry. "Lee, I've already told everyone we were switching to your TPA. How can you do this?" I explained that the RFP did not allow us to present the solution that he recognized his department needed (which was our differentiated, meaningful value). The RFP attempted to force us to be like our competitors, which would lead to a decision based on low price for perceived same services.

He asked us to set aside the RFP and not bow out just yet. He invited us to come to their corporate offices to present our solution to his team and the procurement officers. I agreed. Our presentation day was scheduled for the day after the Super Bowl, which is significant because this company was one of the biggest sponsors of that event.

The Unexpected Reaction

During the presentation, we demonstrated our online technology, explained our service model, and shared our approach to pricing. Just as I finished the presentation, the program manager stood up, put his arms up in the air, and yelled "Touchdown!" All at once, the procurement team dropped their heads because their buying matrix decision process had just imploded. I was stunned by what I had just witnessed. I had never experienced anything like this in my sales career.

After the presentation, we were asked to write a statement of work based on what we believed was the right solution for them. This allowed us to position our differentiators. The RFP never saw the light of day again and we won the deal with no negotiation on price. To this day, the competitors are probably still wondering about the status of that RFP.

Had we responded to the RFP, there is no way we would have won. It did not allow us to present any of our differentiated aspects. The only chance we had to win was to disrupt the buying process in such a way that we could position our differentiators. Having met with the program manager several times, we had effectively positioned those in a meaningful way, which gave us the tools to disrupt the process. Effective sales differentiation necessitates disruption of buyer matrix thinking through *HOW you sell*. If you aren't the low-price provider, a buyer's matrix is your enemy. Sales differentiation provides the tools to ensure your solution won't fit in the grid.

Author the RFP

Not every sales pursuit story ends like that one. Sometimes an RFP will be the way to handle the provider selection process. That doesn't mean the opportunity for sales differentiation through *HOW you sell* is lost. Why not create an RFP template for your buyers to use for provider evaluation?

Most salespeople, when they hear a company buys through RFP, make the mistake of waiting for it to arrive just as I did. Unless you have the relationship described in the earlier story, changing the RFP scope once it has been formulated is very difficult. Providing an RFP template is an added way to differentiate yourself and ensure that the buyer asks the right questions in the document.

Remember from prior chapters, they do not know how to buy what you are selling. You have a broader expertise in the spectrum of available solutions. You also know how to procure your solution more effectively than they do. You know what questions to ask and the key consideration points when making a decision. Buyers think they know more than you, but that is rarely the case. Plus, it takes time to write a comprehensive RFP. These points give you the opportunity to differentiate yourself when buyers require an RFP to explore a provider change.

Develop an RFP template as if you were the one looking to procure the solution you sell. Make it cosmetically attractive, so that a client can use it with little or no modification. Be sure to ask questions that position your differentiators and lock out the competition. For example, if you have an office in the cities in which they operate, and your competitors do not, include a question about locations as that highlights your breadth and differentiates you.

Some will use your RFP template exactly as it was provided to them. Over the years, I've had some buyers send out the template without even updating the footer where it says, "Insert your company name here." Others will pull questions from it and incorporate them into their own RFP. Most important to keep in mind is that whether they use it or not, you've differentiated *HOW you sell* just by offering it! You've taken strategic steps to differentiate in a process designed to commoditize you.

When you hear that a buyer is using an RFP for the selection decision process, rather than agreeing to wait for the RFP to arrive, say:

> "Thank you for sharing that with me. We recognize how difficult and time consuming it is to put together a comprehensive RFP that explores all the important decision elements. We have developed an RFP template you can use to gather information and evaluate potential providers. Clients find this tool very helpful. Would you like me to email it to you?"

By offering the RFP template, there are five wonderful *HOW you sell* sales differentiation benefits.

1. The RFP process will be shorter as the buyer doesn't have to develop the RFP from scratch.
2. The RFP scope and the needs you identified with the buyer will be aligned.
3. Your buyer sees you as helpful, a key differentiator, which reinforces the impression made earlier to intrigue her.
4. You (and your employer) demonstrated expertise in this arena, another important differentiator, which is heavily impactful in buyer decision-making.
5. Your differentiators are positioned in the questions that a procurement-written RFP would not necessarily include.

Be Picky!

It's also important to remember that there is no law requiring you to respond to every RFP that crosses your desk. You have the right to say no, which is the correct decision in some circumstances. If you aren't the low-price provider and you have no relationship with the account, how can you possibly win the deal at the prices you want in an RFP process? You can't and won't. Therefore, responding to countless RFPs under these conditions wastes time and resources, while yielding nothing but losses.

As much as you may want to believe the RFP you just received is a genuine opportunity, it may be nothing more than a sales mirage.

Remember, we all get the same number of hours in our days. Question every task to determine if it is the best use of time at that moment. The most effective salespeople are those who constantly ask themselves that question.

In the drug-testing story, we estimated we would have had to invest more than a hundred hours to respond to an RFP that we were destined to lose. Multiply those hours over the number of accounts that buy through RFP and consider the potential lost selling time and wasted resources.

Issuance of an RFP is not necessarily a commitment to change providers. Some companies require that they source their business every "x" number of years. Just like a salesperson's success is based on achievement of her sales quota, procurement's quota is often based on cost reduction. The RFP that arrived in your inbox could very well be their attempt to put the squeeze on the current provider, so they can show some savings. As much as you may want to believe the RFP you just received is a genuine opportunity, it may be nothing more than a sales mirage.

Three Ways to Handle RFPs

Many salespeople think they have two options when they receive an RFP. One is to respond to it. The other is to toss it in the trash. Few realize they have a third option which can also differentiate them through *HOW you sell*. What if you called the procurement agent and had a conversation that sounded like this:

> "Hi, I'm Lee Salz with XYZ Services. I just received your RFP in my email. Thank you for including us in your process. May I ask you a few questions, so we can determine if it makes sense for us to respond to it? As you can imagine, we receive many RFPs and are very selective when determining to which ones we respond. Do you have a few minutes now to discuss our questions?"

With that said, one of a few things can happen. The procurement agent could agree to answer your questions. Or he could say, "Fill out the RFP or not. It's up to you." My vote is to decline any RFP when the procurement agent won't allow you to ask questions of him. How can you possibly have a fighting chance to win the deal at the prices you want if he won't speak with you (unless you are the low-price provider)?

With permission granted, ask questions that help you determine if you are positioned to win. Questions to consider asking include:

- How did you get our name for inclusion in this process?
- Why is this RFP being administered now?
- Have you definitively decided to change providers?
- What criteria will be used to evaluate the RFPs?
- What departments will be involved in evaluating the RFPs?
- How will the final selection decision be made?
- What are the steps of the process after the RFP is submitted?
- Will we have an opportunity to present to the stakeholders?

Also, I suggest asking scope questions that you need answered, so you can appropriately respond to the RFP. These are very specific questions about the buyer's requirements that procurement can rarely answer alone. This strategy helps to get the "Wizard out from behind the curtain." This gets the Decision Influencers you want to engage involved early in the process. Asking insightful questions could lead to procurement's internal client getting directly involved with you. Bingo!

Asking these questions when receiving an RFP differentiate *HOW you sell*, as you've demonstrated expertise and care while also showing that your company is not desperate for the deal. Sales differentiation gives you the tools to disrupt a buying process that you are not positioned to win at the prices you want.

SALES DIFFERENTIATION CONCEPT #15

Sales differentiation enables buying process disruption.

CHAPTER 16

BUYER OBJECTIONS

An Opportunity for Sales Differentiation

O*bjections!* The mere word "objection" sends shivers down the spines of salespeople. In a courtroom, a lawyer shouts, "I object!" to communicate disagreement with information that has been presented. That's the same message salespeople hear when their Decision Influencers voice disagreement. "I object!" The way salespeople handle that situation determines whether the deal moves forward or dies right at that moment.

During my sales differentiation talks, I ask audiences a fill-in-the-blank question:

"Salespeople should _____ objections."

To a person, the answer shouted out is always "overcome" as that is the traditional way salespeople have been taught to view these disparities. However, that approach is flawed. Salespeople say one of their most compelling differentiators is their ability to build relationships. But how can you build relationships while overcoming objections? It won't work!

Illogical Sales Strategy

Let's dissect this. Salespeople say they overcome objections *and* build relationships. It is completely illogical to have a sales philosophy that says you do those two things.

If you are a salesperson who perceives that DIs present objections, you prepare for every buyer encounter like you would for a fight. Then, you pummel your buyers until you win with an expectation of a hug after the battle. It may work that way in professional boxing, but not in sales. Carnage during the sales process can, and often does, carry over post-sale. The impression made before the sale is directly related to what a DI expects after the sale.

Salespeople think of objecting as fighting because they're hearing the DI say no without necessarily using the word. The sole tool many salespeople have in their toolbox is to attempt to overcome the objection—to turn no into yes.

Because the expression "overcome objections" is so pervasive in sales, that's how most salespeople perceive deal obstacles. Your goal, since you are reading a book on sales differentiation, is to positively stand out from the competition. *HOW you sell* offers many opportunities to do so even when there are deal obstacles.

Deal Obstacles

When salespeople encounter deal obstacles, they are at a crossroads. One path they can take is to "overcome objections." That's a treacherous route, as mentioned before. Salespeople don't often recognize that there is a second path—one that differentiates *HOW you sell.* That path leads salespeople to view those deal obstacles not as "objections" but rather as "concerns."

Salespeople who perceive these deal obstacles as concerns don't hear "fight." They hear "help me." They seek to help the DI resolve their concerns. Sales differentiation replaces the "overcome" tool with a "res-olution" one.

Resolve concerns versus overcome objections may seem like a subtle distinction . . . and those expressions may very well be. However, in win/loss analyses, it's the little things that affect a DI's decision from whom she will buy. The decision differences were often subtle and this philo-sophical shift in *HOW you sell* could give you the differentiated edge over the competition.

Conversely, the philosophies behind overcome objections and resolve concerns could not be more diametrically opposed. If you're using a con-cern resolution tool, it means you recognize the need to sit on the same side of the desk and help work through the concern, not sit across from the DI, ready for a fight.

Eradicating Deal Obstacles

There's an old expression. "An ounce of prevention is worth a pound of cure." This expression is commonly a reference to personal health, en-couraging people to eat well and exercise rather than fight disease later. It is also used to encourage people to manage their money rather than fight to get out of debt. In sales, this saying applies to deal obstacles.

What has been described thus far has been a philosophical shift in the approach to handling deal obstacles through *HOW you sell* sales differen-tiation. Those strategies would be described as a pound of cure. What if we could prevent those deal obstacles from occurring?

For example, if you know that more than 50 percent of the time DIs share a set of concerns, why would you ever let them come up? When buyers share concerns, salespeople respond to them. "Respond," by its very definition, is a de-fensive position. In that mode, you are defending the sale, which is not where you want to be, given

Another opportunity you have to differentiate yourself with *HOW you sell* is to proactively address concerns *before* they arise.

the goal of winning deals at the prices you want. It's a fact: Those who ask the questions control the conversation. When DIs raise concerns, they are in control of the deal, not you.

Another opportunity you have to differentiate yourself with *HOW you sell* is to proactively address concerns *before* they arise. There isn't a magic formula to eliminate concerns, nor are you taping a buyer's mouth shut. What needs to occur is for you to get inside the minds of your buyers and think like them for a moment. Ask yourself:

What are the common concerns on the minds of my buyers?

The Big Question DIs Ask Prematurely

Regardless of *WHAT you sell*—products, services, technology, or software as a service—there is a burning question that DIs want answered. Whether you sell to businesses or consumers, this pressing question is in the forefront of their minds. It doesn't matter if you are selling in Chicago, London, or Tel Aviv; they want this question answered before salespeople should answer it.

The burning question: *How much is it?*

The challenge salespeople face is that they are asked for pricing prematurely. It's asked before they have been able to position meaningful value, which makes the question a deal obstacle. When a salesperson is asked about pricing, she has only two options and neither of them position her to win the deal at the price she wants.

If the salesperson answers the question, she loses. The conversation with the buyer becomes laser-focused on price. Unless you are selling for the low-price provider and price is your differentiator, sharing the price prematurely is a surefire way to lose the deal.

If the salesperson refuses to answer the price question, she also loses. The buyer becomes irritated since the salesperson hasn't answered the question. The conversation takes a contentious tone, which makes for a very short call or meeting. Salespeople have only two response choices when premature pricing requests occur—tell them or not tell them—and both lead to a high likelihood of not getting the deal.

What these two flawed choices tell salespeople is that another strategy is needed to handle premature pricing requests. This type of deal obstacle puts salespeople in a reactionary mode—a defensive posture. They are caught on their heels and come across as defensive with their responses.

Unless what you are offering is free, you know that every DI you encounter has the price question on the brain. You know they want to know it. You know it will come up. Set the stage for the right time to share that information. Why let the price question come up prematurely and derail your deal?

The Rate Question

Salespeople in the mortgage industry know that the first question they will get from a DI is the pricing question. It comes in the form of "a request for their rate." If they share their rate, the person hangs up and calls another mortgage broker to shop for a lower price. If they refuse to tell him the rate, he hangs up the phone angry and never calls back. Again, it's a lose-lose proposition when you allow deal obstacles to control you.

Top mortgage salespeople recognize that there's no answer to the rate question. In the United States, there are many different mortgage loan products. They vary in payback duration and contract structure. Each mortgage loan product has a different rate associated with it. Plus, not all potential mortgagees qualify for all types of loans.

These salespeople recognize that most of their buyers lack the level of mortgage expertise that they do. Their buyers will only know about one product, which is the thirty-year fixed-rate mortgage loan. That product may or may not be the right one for a buyer.

These top mortgage salespeople do not let the deal obstacle get in their way by addressing the rate question before the buyer asks it. They manage the conversation in the following way.

> "I know a big question on your mind is 'what is your rate?' That question would be on my mind too. Most people only know of the thirty-year fixed-rate mortgage product, but there are many different mortgage loan products with different payback durations and contract structures—and not everyone qualifies for all of them.
>
> "We often find that mortgage products other than the thirty-year fixed-rate mortgage can potentially be a better fit for our clients. Like it is for all my clients, selecting a mortgage product is a big decision for you and you want to make sure you make an informed decision. If we can have a ten- to fifteen-minute conversation, this will help us identify the right loan product for you to consider and I can then share the rate for it."

This approach accomplishes several objectives for the mortgage salesperson. First, he has avoided a deal obstacle by bringing up the subject of price before the buyer did. Second, he demonstrated that he understood his buyer and how the buyer was feeling at that moment when he talked about making an informed decision. Third, he demonstrated expertise in the industry by talking about the many mortgage product options and pointing out that not everyone qualifies for all of them. Finally, he further differentiated himself from competitors who would cough up the rate the moment the buyer asked for it. In short, he differentiated himself using *HOW you sell*.

No Answer to the Question

How much is a house . . . a car . . . a computer . . . a tablet . . . a washing machine . . . cleaning services? None of those questions can be answered without first acquiring information from the buyer. Yet, that doesn't prevent buyers from requesting a price prematurely. By proactively addressing the pricing question, you have the opportunity to demonstrate expertise and differentiate yourself in *HOW you sell*.

The example was from the mortgage industry, but you could easily tailor the approach for your sale based on this template:

> By proactively addressing the pricing question, you have the opportunity to demonstrate expertise and differentiate yourself in *HOW you sell*.

"I know a big question on your mind is price. That question would be on my mind too. As you might imagine, there are several factors that affect pricing for what we offer. If I can ask you a few questions, that will allow me to provide the right pricing for you. Is that okay?"

This sales differentiation strategy provides several benefits:

- You've proactively addressed price before it came up.
- You've demonstrated that you understand your buyer and appreciate a burning question on her mind.
- You've explained that providing a price is not as simple as tossing out a number.
- You've allowed the buyer to feel he is still in control by asking permission to provide pricing later, but you are really the one in control.
- You've differentiated yourself from the competition through *HOW you sell*.

This sales differentiation strategy isn't only designed to handle premature pricing requests. It can be (and should be) used to proactively address other potential deal obstacles.

For example, if you know that your price is rarely the lowest, don't wait for it to become a concern when the buyer reads your proposal like the snow contractor did in Chapter 8. Develop a positioning expression that differentiates you and share it as part of the conversation with the buyer early in the process. You could say something such as:

> "I'll tell you upfront that we are never the lowest price for this. Yet, we have over a thousand clients who see the value in what we have to offer. Today, I'll share with you differences our clients appreciate and you can decide if it those differences are meaningful to you."

Rather than have a sales strategy based on crossing your fingers hoping that the buyer isn't educated on market prices, you've proactively positioned that there is value in what you have to offer. Based on your statement regarding your number of clients, it communicates that others have perceived meaningful value and bought from your company. As discussed in Chapter 1, you left the determination of "best" to the buyer based on the differentiated value you will share.

Turning a Shortcoming into a Positive Differentiator

If you know that buyers are concerned with your size, location, or some other aspect of your company, don't bury your head in the sand and pray for the topics not to come up. Develop a positive story that differentiates you from the competition and leads the buyer to want to do business with you.

A client of mine in the oil and gas industry maintained confidentiality agreements with each of its clients—and "confidentiality" is a strong differentiator for them. Those agreements prohibited them from sharing the names of the companies for which they provided services. Confidentiality is a great benefit because the services provided by this firm address a highly sensitive aspect of these companies. Their clients appreciate confidentiality, but this also can also be a deal obstacle.

At some point in a sales conversation, they are going to be asked by a DI to share client names. If they answer the question, they violate the confidentiality provisions of the contract and risk losing the client or being sued. If they don't tell them the client names, they appear defensive in their posturing. Either scenario is again a lose-lose proposition. They also lose the positive story associated with this differentiator.

As part of their sales differentiation strategy, we developed an approach to proactively address client confidentiality early in the initial meeting to ensure buyers didn't raise the question.

> "A question probably on your mind is, 'Who are we providing these services to?' I'd be wondering that as well. One of the aspects that our clients appreciate about our firm is confidentiality, given the sensitive nature of what we do. When we contract to provide services to our clients, we never share their names. You would have that same benefit which reduces your risk and protects your business."

Similar to the premature price request strategy, their salespeople demonstrate an understanding of their clients, expertise in their industry, and position a meaningful differentiator. If they wait for a buyer to ask who their clients are, the differentiator becomes difficult to position because the salespeople come across as defensive.

By proactively addressing concerns, salespeople demonstrate expertise as they show they understand what is on the minds of their DIs. As they communicate their concern for the potential client, they create meaningful differentiation in *HOW you sell*.

Figure 16-1 presents the ten most common deal obstacles and the process to best resolve them. Collaborate with your team to work through the exercise by surfacing best practices for resolution.

FIGURE 16-1: 10 Common Deal Obstacles with Resolution Strategies

DEAL OBSTACLES	When is this most likely to occur? (prospecting, discovery, solution development, contracting)	Why does this occur? (bad experience with another provider, does not meet target client criteria, wrong DI, etc.)	When is the best time to address it? (before it arises or when it arises)	What will you ask, say, and do to remove the deal obstacle?
How much is it?				
I've never heard of your company.				
We are concerned about your size.				
This is not a priority right now.				
I don't have the authority to make this decision.				
I'm concerned about the ramifications of your solution not working properly.				
We don't want to change our process to change providers.				
We want to conduct a pilot before agreeing to a full change.				
We must buy through an RFP.				
Your price is too high.				

In a competitive sales environment, salespeople must take advantage of every opportunity to differentiate themselves. How they handle deal obstacles is another way they differentiate themselves in *HOW you sell.*

SALES DIFFERENTIATION CONCEPT #16

Differentiate yourself by addressing buyer concerns before they arise.

CHAPTER 17

LAST CHANCE TO DIFFERENTIATE
WITH YOUR BUYER

For the last six months, you've been chasing the ABC Business Solutions account. You've had multiple meetings with the key Decision Influencers and they are close to selecting a provider. The decision lies between your company and two others. The competition is fierce, but you think you are in the driver's seat for this deal. Today, at 11:00 a.m., you receive an email from the procurement agent, asking that you provide her with three references. How will you handle this request?

Many salespeople, upon receiving a request for references, "ring the bell" and celebrate victory. "They're asking for references! We're getting the deal!" Some salespeople even update their CRM, based on that request, to an "award." These salespeople think the request for references is a rubber stamp of a victory and nothing more than a rote task to complete. In their minds, the key to success is speed to respond. They quickly send three references back to the procurement agent—the same three they always use.

"Whew! Mission accomplished! They wanted three references and I got it done . . . names and phone numbers of happy clients." What these salespeople don't realize is that the competition also received this request and provided three references quickly. They think they see the deal finish line, forgetting that many a salesperson has fallen one step short of winning.

CHAPTER 17

LAST CHANCE TO DIFFERENTIATE WITH YOUR BUYER

For the last six months, you've been chasing the ABC Business Solutions account. You've had multiple meetings with the key Decision Influencers and they are close to selecting a provider. The decision lies between your company and two others. The competition is fierce, but you think you are in the driver's seat for this deal. Today, at 11:00 a.m., you receive an email from the procurement agent, asking that you provide her with three references. How will you handle this request?

Many salespeople, upon receiving a request for references, "ring the bell" and celebrate victory. "They're asking for references! We're getting the deal!" Some salespeople even update their CRM, based on that request, to an "award." These salespeople think the request for references is a rubber stamp of a victory and nothing more than a rote task to complete. In their minds, the key to success is speed to respond. They quickly send three references back to the procurement agent—the same three they always use.

"Whew! Mission accomplished! They wanted three references and I got it done . . . names and phone numbers of happy clients." What these salespeople don't realize is that the competition also received this request and provided three references quickly. They think they see the deal finish line, forgetting that many a salesperson has fallen one step short of winning.

147

The Major Disconnect Between Buyer and Seller

Of all the steps that buyers go through when making a purchase decision, I've found the request for references to be the one that is most misunderstood by salespeople. Salespeople think that this is just a standard part of due diligence. Some use the term "rubber stamp" to refer to a contract award, but that's not at all how buyers view it.

Why do buyers request references? Webster's defines "reference" as someone who can make a statement about a person's qualifications, character, and dependability. Buyers look at the reference step as their final opportunity to validate the messages they have been hearing from potential providers.

In essence, DIs are searching to ascertain whether a provider can deliver on the promises made by salespeople. Can the provider handle an account of this size? Are they actually that fast? Or that accurate? Is the service as good as they described? In other words, despite marketing literature and sales speak preaching "best," buyers want to hear from those who already purchased from your company before making their decision.

Why is this validation step so important to DIs? Decision-making carries with it the dangers of risk. The person who signs off on changing providers or outsourcing for the first time is accountable for that decision. If something goes wrong, the search for a scapegoat begins. The one who made the decision to change is in jeopardy. Depending upon the severity of the issues, a promotion could be at stake or maybe even someone's job. Fear of change is a common reason why buyers decide to stay with their current solution.

Coming back to my point about the disconnect concerning the request for references, salespeople see the request as a task while DIs view this as a critical validation step. The request for references is a common part of the buyer decision-making process. However, few salespeople use the reference stage as one final opportunity to differentiate themselves—to stand out from the competition by providing meaningful value in

HOW you sell. After all, after the reference validation step, a decision will be made. Will you win the deal at the prices you want?

Differentiation Through Reference Management

When I talk with salespeople, one of their most common gripes is that they are selling something often perceived as a commodity. They cite price as their biggest challenge. Right behind that, they lament about their inability to differentiate in *WHAT you sell.* They commonly forget they have opportunities to differentiate based on *HOW you sell*—in this case, through the handling of the request for references.

When I ask salespeople if they would like to learn an easy way to get a competitive edge, they are all ears. After I share with them that they can differentiate themselves through the handling of a request for references, they look at me in shock. They cannot believe they have been missing out on this opportunity.

It's the little things that winning salespeople do that keep them on top. They look at every interaction with buyers as an opportunity to provide meaningful value that the competition does not. Given the understanding you now have of what buyers are attempting to accomplish through the request for references, how can you differentiate yourself in this step? While the competing salespeople are going to handle the request for references as a task, you have an opportunity to provide a meaningful, differentiated experience.

> While the competing salespeople are going to handle the request for references as a task, you have an opportunity to provide a meaningful, differentiated experience.

Putting This Strategy into Practice

In the story I shared, I mentioned that upon receiving this request, the salesperson sent the same three references for this account that he has always used. Using the same references over and over again is a common sales approach, but not a best practice. The reason most salespeople use the same ones repeatedly is that they only have three in their quiver. The first step to using the request for references as a sales differentiation opportunity is to put together a client reference portfolio.

Think about what your buyers usually want to validate through conversations with your clients. In some cases, they want to hear about the service experiences. In others, there are geographic concerns. Some are concerned about size—too big or too little. One concern that's common among buyers is the transition process, commonly referred to as "client onboarding" or "implementation." They want to learn from other people's experiences with your company.

Put together a list of the aspects that buyers want to validate through references. Examples include: location, size, quality, speed, service, and onboarding. Those are just a few examples, not a comprehensive list.

Salespeople can't differentiate through reference selection unless they have a portfolio to search for the right ones to align with a specific deal. Given the factors you have identified that buyers want to validate through references, assemble a portfolio of clients who can speak to those aspects. Ideally, the portfolio should have a minimum of twenty-five client references in it to avoid reference exhaustion. There are only so many times per month that one of your clients will agree to serve as a reference.

A company is not a reference. Each of the DIs at a company are reference candidates. That means the same company can be represented multiple times in the portfolio given the many relationships that have been developed.

Handling the Reference Request

Many salespeople take the request for references as marching orders. "They want three references. I'll get them three references." To differentiate

HOW you sell, don't just accept the request, but rather ask two questions of the requestor:

> "So that I can provide you with the right clients to talk with, what are you hoping to learn during these conversations?
> Who will be contacting the references?"

The answers to these questions will affect who you provide as references. Knowing that they want to better understand the service experience allows you to connect them with clients of yours who can speak to that. Understanding that they want to learn more about the way in which you manage accounts gives you the opportunity to select those who can speak to your account management approach.

The second question, asking who will be making the reference phone calls, allows you to align roles. If a CFO is going to be the one making the calls, wouldn't it be beneficial to your buyer if you connected them with a CFO reference, so they can talk about aspects most important to CFOs?

Even if the reference requestor can't (or won't) provide you with answers to those two questions, you have demonstrated that you care about what they are trying to accomplish. And "care" can be the differentiator that pushes you across the finish line.

In addition to the answers to those two requests for guidance in selecting the right references, reflect on your experiences with the account's Decision Influencers. What were their concerns or hesitations in moving forward with your company? If they were worried about speed, provide them with a reference who can speak to that point. The answer to the concerns and hesitations question is the third component when selecting references for this deal.

More Than Name, Rank, and Serial Number

In the aforementioned story, the salesperson only provided the name and phone number for the references, which is what most salespeople do. Others include an email address as well. Given the goal of differentiating *HOW you sell*, let the competition send that basic information. You are going to do something valuably different.

Certainly, you will provide name and title as well as phone number and email address. However, since a buyer's process of reference evaluation is often undefined, salespeople can differentiate themselves by providing a description for the requestor that explains what the reference can address.

In a short narrative, explain the reference's role in his company, how you work with him, and for what aspects he can serve as a reference. This connects the dots based on what the buyer wants to accomplish through reference conversations. It also helps the buyer have the conversations he needs to have to quickly validate the important aspects, while again communicating your care and understanding of their process. Here is an example of that communication:

> Brandon Avery is the Vice President of Operations for XYX Corporation. We've been providing services to them for seven years. Brandon has been the one managing the relationship between our two companies. He can speak to the creative solutions we've brought forward to help them address the same challenges you've mentioned, such as limited space and sparse resources.
>
> My suggestion is to email him to schedule a phone conversation. His email address is brandon@xyzcorporation.com and his phone number is (xxx) xxx-xxxx.
>
> I've told him to expect to hear from you. I hope you find the conversation helpful.

What you have just read is not a message buyers are accustomed to receiving from salespeople. It demonstrates that you and your company care about the reference experience, which is a meaningful differentiator.

Notice the last line of the sample response to the request for references. We have shared with the reference requestor that our client is expecting to hear from him. Many a deal has been lost due to a buyer citing the reference experience as the reason why they selected an alternative provider.

One cause of a poor reference experience is not managing the client reference side of the equation. A common misstep is not notifying the reference that a prospective client will be contacting him. Some of your clients may have given you *carte blanche* to use them as a reference any time. It's a trap! Don't fall into it.

Coaching Your Client Reference

If you don't notify your client that someone is calling him to discuss your company, there is the possibility he won't be available—and you might not know that he is unavailable for the call. The request from your prospective buyer goes unreturned and that reflects negatively on you.

Plus, no provider is perfect. Perhaps your company dropped the ball for this client last week and your usually supportive contact does not want to have a reference conversation right now.

Further complicating the reference process: *Most people don't know how to serve as a reference.* There is no training offered for that function. Even with the best intentions, people don't always know what to say that will be helpful to the conversation so that you win the deal at the prices you want. References need a salesperson's coaching to effectively serve in this deal-critical capacity.

A great way to burn a relationship with a happy client is to surprise them with a reference's phone call. No one likes to be blindsided or unprepared—even those who have given you *carte blanche*. An unprepared reference reflects negatively on the provider.

Assuming you already have permission to use a client as a reference, send your client an email letting him know that a prospective buyer will be contacting him. Share with him who will be calling and what he wants to learn during the conversation. Don't be afraid to coach him. After all, he is not trained to sell for you.

Also, be sure to ask your client to discuss the ways in which you personally provide value to the account beyond what your company brings to bear. In other words, notify your client and prepare him to be the reference you need as part of your sales differentiation strategy. Here is an example of this communication:

> Thank you for agreeing to serve as a reference for us. Joseph Marlo will be contacting you. I've given him both your email address and phone number but suggested that he email you to arrange for a phone conversation.
>
> Joseph (he goes by his full name) Regina is the vice president of operations for ABC Business Solutions. He and his colleagues are interested in the same program we have been providing to you for seven years. Please speak to the creative solutions we've provided to help you address the challenges of limited space and sparse resources as he has the same issues.
>
> Just as I am for your account, I would be their account manager. When you talk with Joseph, please be sure to share your experiences with me as your account manager. Mention my responsiveness and the proactive ways in which I manage your account.
>
> Thank you again for your help.

The emails sent to the client reference and the prospective buyer ensure that the buyer accomplishes his validation goals. These emails help your buyer have an outstanding experience that differentiates you.

Reference Management Batting Average

Measurement of strategy effectiveness is always important. References play an important role in a buyer's decision-making process so you will want to monitor performance. The data helps with future reference selection processes, allowing you to pick the right ones leading you to win the deal.

Track your account wins and losses relative to the references selected for them. For example, you may discover that 96 percent of the time, when using David Harmon as a reference, you win the account, indicating that you should continue using him for that function.

However, when Jamie Stevens is asked to serve as a reference, you only win 46 percent of the time. Perhaps she needs more coaching or is not as happy with your company as you thought. In any case, some investigation is needed regarding the relationship with Jamie. You don't know who the rock star references are or where potential issues reside if you aren't tracking performance.

In a competitive selling landscape, salespeople need to use every opportunity they have to differentiate themselves. Every little bit of differentiation gives them an additional edge pushing them over the top. Reference management is your last opportunity to provide meaningful, differentiated value in *HOW you sell* before the decision is final.

SALES DIFFERENTIATION CONCEPT #17

The request for references is your last chance to differentiate with a buyer. Don't miss it.

CHAPTER 18

KEEPING THE STRATEGY FRESH

In Chapter 15, I shared the story of the workplace drug testing TPA and the sales differentiation strategy we used to win the deal at the prices we wanted. The RFP was cast aside, and we were awarded the contract. However, that wasn't the end of that TPA's sales differentiation story.

For about two years, we were able to use the sales differentiation strategy founded in technology, service, and open-book pricing to win more deals at the prices we wanted. However, the competition quickly took note of our success and began following suit. They copied our technology and emulated our service model.

We had no choice but to go back to the sales differentiation drawing board. We analyzed the industry and found a buyer frustration point from which we could develop our next generation sales differentiation strategy.

Reinventing Ourselves

While this division's focus was drug testing, our other division provided background screening services, usually to the same clients. It was not uncommon to find twenty or more background screening providers delivering services for a single company. Why would employers use so many background check companies for pre-employment screening? The provider decision for background screening was often decentralized, which opened the door for all these service providers. However, senior executives came to recognize that decentralized management of background screening (and drug testing) was costly, inefficient, and left the company vulnerable to inconsistent hiring and screening practices.

This led to a new sales differentiation opportunity, which was to offer both drug testing and background screening services under one umbrella called "employment screening."

The approach made a lot of sense. There were two barriers of entry into a company: a drug test and a background check. Why not have one provider serve as the main point of contact for all employment screening needs? That provider could provide a consolidated, detailed invoice for all services, a single report for each applicant including both the drug test and background screening results.

Seemingly overnight, this effective sales differentiation strategy shifted to a marketplace requirement. All the industry players began offering both services in a very similar fashion. Another wave of salespeople arguing "best" began, which again led to price erosion.

Changing the Game

One of our competitors went into "stealth mode" and changed the entire playing field. Companies began adopting Applicant Tracking Systems (ATS) to manage candidate pools and hiring processes. This competitor developed exclusive agreements with ATS companies and developed integrations with them. Those integrations allowed them to position a differentiated story of being able to order and receive employment screening reports within the ATS. Rather than fight over which provider offered the best service, this company changed the entire employment screening conversation with a strategy that led to tremendous success by locking out the competition.

Over time, the exclusivity agreements with the ATS companies lapsed and competitors also developed these integrations. While all the industry players made huge investments in technology to support their clients, the fast growth of the industry and provider consolidation through acquisition led to a degradation of service.

The industry again faced a price war and the battle for differentiation raged on. As the industry players were painfully reminded, price is the ultimate decision-factor in the absence of differentiation. Interestingly, the evolution described didn't take place over twenty or fifty years. It took place in less than ten years.

Thus, the sales differentiation strategy you develop for your company is for now, but it needs to be regularly revisited to make sure that it is still effective. The game will change, and you must change with it to continue winning deals at the prices you want. A great example of this point is in the smartphone industry.

Email on the Go!

I was one of the first people in the United States to own a Blackberry. I'll never forget the first conversation I had with the Blackberry salesperson. He said, "Lee, get this . . . email on the go! People will be able to send you a message and you will be able to send a response back on the device. How cool is that?! Forget those pagers that show you a phone number and you have to call the person to see what they want. You'll have two-way communication at your fingertips."

This story certainly was different which is why I had a Blackberry strapped to my belt the very first day the devices were available in the United States. Imagine that same salesperson calling on me today with that same "differentiated" story to sell me a Blackberry. "Email on the go!" I'd think he was crazy. Why? The smartphone is now an accepted part of the business professional's toolkit. All of them have that function. We bought into the "email on the go" concept long ago. What we need help determining is the right device for us given that the market is flooded with devices that have varying features, functions, and price points.

Constant Change

There is much debate on the future of the sales profession. *What's to become of salespeople?* No one has a crystal ball telling them what the future holds. But there are steps salespeople can and should take, not only to avoid extinction, but to continue to dominate the sales game. Quite frankly, the salesperson in the Blackberry story deserves to fall to the perils of extinction for failing to evolve with his buyers. Salespeople need to be on a never-ending quest to provide meaningful value in both *WHAT you sell* and *HOW you sell*.

> Every industry goes through changes. Not some, but all of them do!

Every industry goes through changes. Not some, all of them do! No industry is immune. What people buy. How people buy. Why people buy. Which people buy. When people buy. The answers are evolutionary, which means your sales differentiation strategy needs to evolve as well.

Yoda Salespeople

Look at the new car industry. Not long ago, new car salespeople were viewed as Yoda, the wise, all-knowing being in *Star Wars*. Those salespeople knew everything about the features, functions, rebates, and deals for the cars they sold. Buyers relied on salespeople to share their wisdom so they could make educated car-purchase decisions. There was no other way to find out that information.

We don't need new car salespeople to play the "Yoda role" anymore. The internet puts every bit of information (and even more than what the salespeople shared) at our fingertips. Buyers have become more educated. That means *HOW you sell* needs to evolve. People may think they are educated about the car buying process, but many need a salesperson's expertise to help them make the right decision. Remember the Forrester statistic from the second chapter: "74 percent of buyers conduct more than half of their research online before talking with a salesperson."

If you are a new car salesperson clinging to the "Yoda past" and using the same selling approach today that you used yesterday, I'm guessing that you probably aren't selling as many cars as you did previously. You've not adapted your approach to the changes in the buying process—and that puts you at risk. Rather than come to the showroom for starters, often buyers are beginning the process with you by phone after they have researched vehicles online. That means you need to provide meaningful value telephonically or be adept at attracting buyers to come to the showroom.

According to J.D. Power and Associates, in 2005 the average car buyer visited 4.5 dealerships before making a purchase. Today, she visits an average of 1.4. How people buy cars has changed, which means salespeople need to change with it. This dynamic should not be a surprise given Forrester's findings.

What is also interesting is a 2016 report from *Autotrader* that said 72 percent of buyers would visit dealerships more often if the buying process was improved. This is certainly an opportunity to create meaningful value in *HOW you sell*.

Buyer Evolution

Another aspect that evolves: what cars people buy. When gas prices are high, they want efficient vehicles. When gas prices are low, they are more flexible with their options. Salespeople need to be on top of the trends that affect buying decisions, so they continue to be seen as an expert resource.

The internet hasn't just impacted new car salespeople. It has changed selling for all salespeople in all industries. Salespeople used to be able to show up on a Decision Influencer's doorstep and ask, "What is it you do here?" Given that the only way to learn that information was to ask, DIs were often willing to share it. Ask that question today and you will quickly be shown the door.

If someone is willing to meet with you, they expect meaningful value from that interaction. That gives you the opportunity to differentiate. However, what was considered meaningful value to buyers yesterday is different today and will likely be different tomorrow.

While I wish I could tell you that the sales differentiation strategy you develop will last forever, it won't. The differentiated, meaningful value associated with *WHAT you sell* and *HOW you sell* evolves—and so must your sales differentiation strategy. How often it changes depends on the speed of change in your industry. Revisit your sales differentiation strategy periodically. When conducting your sales differentiation strategy checkup, ask these questions:

- Do Decision Influencers still care about the differentiated aspects in *WHAT you sell*?
- Are those aspects still different or has the competition mirrored you?
- Is there something different you can do to provide more meaningful value to your DIs?
- Are there new differentiation opportunities in *WHAT you sell*?
- Are there ways you can further differentiate yourself?
- Are you still winning deals at the prices you want?

SALES DIFFERENTIATION CONCEPT #18

Sales differentiation is a moment in time, not a permanent state.

CHAPTER 19

THE IRREFUTABLE DIFFERENTIATOR

Throughout this book, I've shared ways in which you can differentiate *WHAT you sell* and *HOW you sell*. There is a final part of your sales differentiation strategy to address that has not been mentioned until now. This component has the potential to be the most powerful differentiator in your toolkit and is part of the *HOW you sell* component of your sales differentiation strategy. It is irrefutably a differentiator and you have total control over its level of value.

The final part of your sales differentiation strategy is YOU!

Salespeople often forget that they play a major role in sales differentiation. Most salespeople can't materially change *WHAT they sell* to differentiate their wares from the competition. As we previously talked about, you can use each phase of the sales process as an opportunity to differentiate, but why not use all the tools available to you? When someone buys from your company, *you* are part of the deal. They can't get you from the competition. The introspective question to be asked:

> "Is the meaningful value you personally bring to the table compelling enough, such that a Decision Influencer would prefer to buy from you instead of your competitors?"

When I conduct sales differentiation workshops, I ask the participants about the value they personally bring to bear for their clients, forgetting for the moment what they sell. That question usually leaves a blank look on their faces, as they have not thought through this essential part of their sales differentiation strategy.

When I ask them to share their personal value differentiation with the group, the most common responses are friendly, honest, accessible, and fast to return calls. "How can you prove any of those to someone with whom you haven't done business?" I ask the groups. The blank stares become raised eyebrows when they recognize they can't.

> Coach your clients, when they serve as references, to talk about the way you manage their accounts and the value you personally bring to bear.

No salesperson tells buyers he is unfriendly, dishonest, inaccessible, and slow to return calls. They all use the same expressions, which aren't differentiators at all. If these are the expressions you use, I'm sorry to be the one to break the news to you, but you sound just like every other salesperson. You've failed to differentiate yourself.

How can you prove that there is more than just lip service behind those expressions? The answer is found in Chapter 17 in the discussion of reference management. Coach your clients, when they serve as references, to talk about the involvement you have with accounts and the value you personally bring to them. That's your way of proving your personal differentiated value to someone considering buying from you. Remember, when you say *best* it's meaningless, but when your clients say it about you, it means everything!

Here are seven ways to incorporate personal value differentiation in *HOW you sell* as part of your overall sales differentiation strategy.

1. Become a Knowledge Resource

Throughout this book, I've shared the foundation point that buyers don't have the expertise that salespeople do in purchasing what they sell. Buyers need your help. They thirst for it! They get frustrated when salespeople don't provide it. Remember, they don't know how to buy what you are selling!

To create personal value differentiation, become the expert resource that you would seek if you were buying *WHAT you sell*.

For buyers to perceive you as that valuable resource and seek your insight, you need to master your products, your industry, the Decision Influencers you sell to, and the competitive landscape.

Some people use the expressions "upstream" and "downstream" to describe the effects on a business process before and after a change. Top salespeople know the impacts of what they sell on the overall organization.

"Upstream" and "downstream" mean that you shouldn't limit your knowledge to just *WHAT you sell* but expand it to include tangent aspects. For example, if you sell televisions, you should not only master your television product knowledge, but also the impact that wiring, internet speed, and other devices have on the buyer's purchase decision.

A salesperson's expertise helps buyers identify and address potential issues. It also helps them identify critical decision points for their business that they could not find on their own.

2. Develop a Network Neighborhood

Many companies have massive client databases. They send clients newsletters or solicitation messages with offers in them. Regardless of what they do, there is an opportunity for you to provide personal value differentiation in *HOW you sell* to your clientele.

Given the objective of being seen as a knowledge resource, you need to be communicating with your community of prospects and clients directly and with regular frequency. Put together an email list of those who are currently buying from you and those who are still prospects. Those two groups comprise your "network neighborhood."

These are people you want to stay in front of, not with a solicitation, but rather with information related to your industry that they will find helpful.

You are providing content to keep them apprised of important happenings as it relates to the synergy between your world and theirs. This helps them in their roles and leads them to see you as a knowledge resource.

The knowledge resource strategy is the same strategy people use, so that they'll be seen as thought leaders on social media. By sharing information, you are perceived as having expertise in that subject area. For example, if you continually share information on baby safety, even though you aren't the author of any of the content, you become viewed as an expert on baby safety.

Some of the best salespeople at leveraging this aspect of personal value differentiation are home real estate agents. One agent in my neighborhood sends a newsletter (not email) at least once per month with information related to home ownership. Sometimes, the mailer is about plumbing; other times, it's about security or lawn care. He also educates on the process to buy and sell a home. In essence, he hits upon the topics that are important to homeowners. I look forward to receiving his newsletter and, should I ever decide to put my home on the market, he is at the top of my list for consideration to be my real estate agent. He has demonstrated subject matter expertise that would be tremendously valuable to me.

As you put together your "network neighborhood" program, determine a sustainable frequency at which you will communicate with the group. Monthly or semi-monthly touches are more than enough for most sale types. Remember, these are not solicitations. Share information related to happenings in your industry—new trends, new solutions, new regulations, etc. Make sure your contact information is included in every communication. You can develop this program easily, professionally, and inexpensively with email systems like Constant Contact.

3. Provide Decision Guidance

Don't keep your knowledge a secret, but also don't lecture buyers and show off. You'll come off like the prototypical salespeople who are peddling their wares.

In Chapter 13, you learned how to develop positioning questions—open-ended queries designed to help buyers think differently about the solutions they have or could have. Rather than lecture, lead buyers to arrive at the right conclusions for their needs. Your foundation message, as discussed in Chapter 12 on word selection, is "help." Help your buyers make the right decisions because you have expertise that they don't.

4. Be Responsive and Anticipate Needs

Think of this as customer service and account management. Customer service comes into play when a client asks you to complete a task, such as providing a report or creating a new user on the website. Account management is the set of proactive actions you take to ensure client delight.

Being responsive is considered table stakes. That's an expectation any DI would have of you. But proactive involvement in the account is a quantifiable way to demonstrate personal value differentiation. Most salespeople wait for their company to provide them with an account management plan. Unfortunately, most companies don't have one. That means you need to develop an account management plan on your own that provides value and makes clients loyal to you.

One example of personal value differentiation in *HOW you sell* through account management comes in the form of providing actionable information, not just data. Anyone can pull a report from their back-office system and email it to a client. If you want to differentiate yourself, don't send data reports. Explain to your client what the data indicates to you and help her adjust her purchasing relationship based on it.

5. Develop Internal Relationships So You Can Solve Issues Fast

Executives often tell me "Jekyll and Hyde" stories about their salespeople. They talk about how effective their salespeople are in working with clients, but internally, they are a nightmare. (I'm sure you just chuckled because you have someone on your sales team who fits this bill.)

Years ago, researchers conducted a study in which CEOs were asked why they bought from one salesperson versus another. Overwhelmingly, they said they bought from the salespeople they believed had the full support of the companies behind them. When, not if, something went wrong, the CEOs wanted to be sure they were working with someone who could get the problem resolved fast.

Despite the "best" marketing language on your website and collateral materials, these executives know no one is flawless. As they consider their buying decision, they eyeball the salespeople attempting to determine which ones can resolve issues quickly.

If you are among the salespeople who are guilty of "Jekyll and Hyde," take the time to fix your missteps and develop internal relationships. We all know that client issues are handled in two ways. There is the set of standard operating procedures (SOPs) that prescribes issue resolution plans. Then, there is the relationship set of plans that always trumps the SOPs. As a salesperson, if you have a relationship with operations, customer service, IT, etc., you can get what your clients need much faster than salespeople who treat their colleagues like garbage. Having strong internal relationships is a very effective personal value differentiator that you should talk about with buyers.

6. Be Genuine

In Chapter 10, I shared the story about the technology education company for which I ran sales. We sold to three segments: corporations, the federal government, and career changers. Our specialized career changer sales team sold to consumers.

That team's job was to help people procure the training they needed to get jobs in information technology. Whether they had little growth opportunity or made too little money where they presently worked, they desired to change their lives. Many were in severe debt. Some wanted to start families or buy cars or homes, which made this an emotional sale. It wasn't about the classes they were taking, but rather the career opportunity they sought for themselves.

For the career changer sales team, I could stack rank my salespeople based on the use of one item. *Tissues!* My top salespeople went through boxes and boxes of tissues. For the lower tier salespeople, however, the box of tissues that was in their office when they began working for me was the same box that was there when they left. Those salespeople never appreciated the emotional part of this sale.

> Salespeople who don't genuinely care about their clients aren't long for the sales profession.

At holiday time, I was always amazed as the postman, UPS, and FedEx delivery people arrived at the office, not to pick up, but rather to drop off gifts from the students to their salespeople. When the program graduates would get new jobs, their first phone call wasn't to their significant others. The calls went to the salespeople that had helped them achieve success through this challenging educational program.

I wish I had magical words to share that would teach salespeople how to be genuine. Fact is, you are or you are not. Try to fake it and buyers will see it a mile away. Salespeople who don't genuinely care about their clients aren't long for the sales profession, but those who do have a wonderful personal value differentiator in their quiver.

Quite frankly, if you aren't passionate about the solutions your company provides or helping the people to whom you are selling, give serious thought to selling for another company or exiting the profession altogether.

Whatever your Decision Influencer's goals are, own them. If the goal is to gain promotions, champion that effort and help them get there. Cost reduction ... efficiency ... increase sales: Whatever their goal, make it yours, too. No one in any situation wants to feel like a number. Everyone wants to feel special and important. That is something you can do by owning your clients' goals and differentiating *HOW you sell*.

Few people put pen to paper and provide that personal touch that shows you care.

One way to demonstrate that you are genuine is with a handwritten note. Today, it is very easy to type an email and click send. Few people put pen to paper and provide that personal touch that shows you care. Care, a personal touch, and being genuine are not only intertwined, but have also become more important as the infusion of technology has rendered business impersonal. All that gives you the opportunity to stand out through personal value differentiation.

7. Help Them with Their Business

During the interactions you have with DIs, you may learn they have challenges and objectives that *WHAT you sell* doesn't address. For example, if you are selling tax services and you learn they have some electrical issues, see if you have a reputable electrical firm to whom you can introduce them. No, you won't make money on that referral, but that's not the goal. If you genuinely care about your clients, help them with their business even if it doesn't mean dollars in your pocket today.

Years ago, I had a salesperson working for me in a company that sold services to the Fortune 1000. We had a very long sales cycle of twelve to eighteen months. Oftentimes, buyers would want to change to us, but were prohibited from doing so for some period of time due to contractual restrictions.

Despite the long sales cycle, this salesperson found ways to demonstrate her personal value differentiation. She helped these executives in other aspects of their business while the clock ticked on their expiring contracts with the competition. When her first child was born, she received gifts from many of these companies. The kicker is that she received these gifts even though they were not yet doing a nickel of business with us.

Between being genuine and helping them with other aspects of the business, she created meaningful value that differentiated her. They looked forward to the day when there would be a revenue relationship—which there eventually was.

While many salespeople search high and low for differences in *WHAT you sell*, look no further than the personal value differentiation component of *HOW you sell*. It could be your key to winning more deals at the prices you want.

SALES DIFFERENTIATION CONCEPT #19

The irrefutable differentiator is *YOU* . . . make it invaluable!

CONCLUSION

Using Sales Differentiation to Get in the Door with Prospects

O ur journey in this book has taken us through the development process of sales differentiation strategy. Using the Sales Differentiation
Universe and two workshops shared in Chapter 5, you identified your
set of compelling differentiators. In Chapter 6, I shared with you the importance of aligning differentiators with the right Decision Influencers
to ensure your sales differentiation strategy resonated. In Chapter 13, you
learned how to develop a communication strategy for your differentiators.

Based on the work you've done, I'm going to teach you an application
of sales differentiation that deals with the toughest challenge salespeople
face: *getting in the door with buyers who say they are happy in their current
circumstance*. I call this application the *"We're Happy Disruption Strategy"*
which helps you open doors with those who say they are happy.

Screaming for Change!

Election season is always a fascinating time in this country. Politicians,
citizens, and the media make their case for change. Yet, come Election Day, despite the pleas for change, more than 90 percent of elected

congressional representatives keep their jobs. Despite people begging for change, these politicians are reelected into office.

When salespeople make prospecting calls, they don't often hear dissatisfaction on the other end of the phone. Anecdotally speaking, when first contacted by a salesperson, more than 90 percent of buyers say they are happy with their current provider. Salespeople are challenged to win more deals at the prices they want when most initial interactions with buyers begin by stating that they are happy with the status quo.

Three Common Resolution Strategies That Don't Work

Traditional sales training has taught salespeople three strategies to handle the "we're happy" deal obstacle. The first is asking permission to call back at a future date.

> *"Would it be okay if I call you back in three months to see if you are still happy?"*

Think about the message heard by the buyer. "If you call back in three months and hear that I am miserable, this will be your greatest day ever." Of course, this is not a healthy way to begin a business relationship.

A second strategy is to pretend you didn't hear them say they are happy and continue pushing your wares. Let's anger the person on the other end of the phone and then expect them to buy from us. Not likely to happen!

A third strategy is innocuous, but also ineffective. It's the "magic wand" technique.

> *"Nobody's perfect, what are three things you would like to have but don't have today?"*

You certainly won't anger someone by asking it. The issue with this strategy is that they don't know about the world of potential solutions at the level that you do. They don't know they could have something different that would be an improvement over what they already have.

What all three of these strategies have in common is that they fail to open the door for you to position your differentiators. With 90 percent of initial buyer interactions beginning with "we're happy," salespeople need an effective strategy to gain buyer interest or risk losing an incalculable number of deals.

Does Happy Mean Happy?

What does it mean when buyers say they are happy? Let's start with what it does not mean. The organization did not conduct a comprehensive survey gauging happiness with the current provider. The sole measure of happiness is that no one is complaining. Thus, when a salesperson calls and the buyer doesn't want to have a conversation on the subject, the easiest route to take is to say, "We're happy." That should make the salesperson go away. At least, that's the buyer's hope.

Buyers who say they are happy are in a static state. They are complacent.

Even though the sole measure of happiness is that no one is complaining, salespeople need to understand the message communicated by the buyer. Buyers who say they are happy are in a static state. They are complacent. When buyers are complacent, they are not receptive to new ideas and solutions. When salespeople try to sell to complacent buyers, their message falls on deaf ears.

Before you can have a meaningful conversation about *WHAT you sell*, buyer complacency needs to be disrupted. Buyers need to be led into a receptive state before salespeople can talk about the solutions their company offers. Only when buyer complacency has been disrupted will a Decision Influencer be willing to learn about a solution that she perceives could be a better alternative.

Opening Doors Through Sales Differentiation

The strategy you are about to learn is designed to accomplish the following six objectives and uses concepts in both *WHAT you sell* and *HOW you sell* that have been presented in this book.

1. Engage the buyer in conversation.
2. Disrupt buyer complacency.
3. Position relevant differentiators.
4. Help a buyer think differently about the solutions he has or could have.
5. Challenge a buyer's beliefs.
6. Evoke a specific call to action (that you set).

With these six objectives in mind, here is an eight-step process that opens doors with so-called "happy buyers."

STEP 1

"I'm not surprised at all by your saying that you're happy. Most of my initial conversations with <u>our current clients</u> began with them saying exactly the same thing.

"May I ask you one question?" *Wait for approval.*

Buyers expect salespeople to become argumentative when they say they are happy. This strategy differentiates *HOW you sell* as you are supportive of their position.

The expression "our current clients" in this first step is underlined to highlight an important subtlety of the strategy. That expression suggests that people who were feeling the same way they do made the switch to your company. It may be subtle, but it works!

STEP 2

"Are you happy or satisfied with your current provider?"

Common response: "What's the difference?"

One of your goals is to lead them into conversation. When a DI asks about the difference between those two expressions, she has begun dialogue with you. That means you are on your way to achieving objective number one.

STEP 3

"If you contrast happy and satisfied with a school environment . . .

"If you are happy, that's like getting an 'A' on a report card. It means that your current provider exceeds your expectations each and every day.

"If you are satisfied, that's like getting a 'C' on a report card. It means your minimum expectations are being met.

"So, coming back to my question: Are you happy or satisfied with your current provider?"

Most will say "satisfied." If so, skip to step 5.

This part of the strategy suggests that they reflect on their provider's performance given the context you have given to the words "happy" and "satisfied." It begins the process of disrupting complacency.

STEP 4

If HAPPY: "That's wonderful to hear. May I ask what your current provider is doing for you that exceeds your expectations?" *Wait for a response.*

"It's interesting to hear that those items exceed your expectations. For us, those are things we do in the normal course of business—things that we would consider getting a 'C' on a report card."

Again, buyers expect salespeople to become combative when they don't give the answer a salesperson wants to hear. Differentiating *HOW you sell*, you convey that you are happy to hear they are happy. This helps to diffuse common negative salesperson perceptions they may have.

STEP 5

"May I share with you why our clients, who felt the same way you did, decided to take a closer look at our company and what they found when they did?" *Wait for approval.*

Remembering that this buyer is in a complacent state, she needs to be led into a receptive state. In step 5, if you change the expression "take a closer look" to "bought from our company," you risk sounding like a typical, pushy salesperson. The door to opportunity with this buyer slams shut. There is a gradual process to leading someone from static to receptive and salespeople need to be sensitive to that.

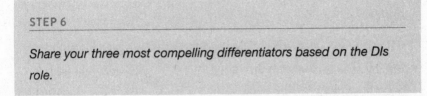

STEP 6

Share your three most compelling differentiators based on the DIs role.

This is the step where both *WHAT you sell* and *HOW you sell* come together. Look back at the portfolio of differentiators you developed in Chapter 5. Contrast those with the Decision Influencer you are contacting and select the three most compelling differentiators based on what would resonate most with this buyer.

Be mindful of what was covered in Chapter 7 relative to giving each differentiator context and meaning. Share the three differentiators in a pithy, yet intriguing fashion. Case studies and client examples are the most effective ways to accomplish that.

STEP 7

"Given what I've just shared with you, do you feel you have the absolute best _____ solution you could have for the dollars you are willing to invest?" *Most will say "no."*

In the blank, insert the description for your solution. For example, if you sell printers, you could say "the absolute best printer solution."

This step of the strategy challenges the buyer's beliefs. Most have not conducted a comprehensive study to determine if the solution they selected is the best one for the dollars they are willing to invest. The question challenges her to think about the solution she has and recognize there could potentially be a better alternative.

STEP 8

"Quite frankly, I don't know if we have something better to offer you. But if you would be willing to _____, perhaps, that will become evident to both of us."

In the blank, insert the call to action you desire as a result of this interaction. It could be to continue the conversation, agree to a meeting, or some other desired outcome.

You may have noticed that I used the word "better" in this strategy. The reason for that is I'm aligning my communication with their perspective. I'm not referring to what I have to sell as "better."

Buyers expect salespeople to be aggressive and do whatever they can to get a sale. Again, you have differentiated *HOW you sell* by taking a step back and acknowledging that you may not have a better solution for them. This creates a positive impression of both the salesperson and the company. Buyers find this approach refreshing. They know a salesperson can't make a believable claim to have a better mousetrap if he doesn't know much about the account.

Reflecting on this strategy, here is what was accomplished:

1. Engaged the buyer in conversation.
2. Disrupted complacency.
3. Positioned relevant differentiators.
4. Helped a buyer think differently about the solutions she has or could have.
5. Challenged a buyer's beliefs.
6. Had a specific call to action (that you set).

This *We're Happy Disruption Strategy* is a combination of sales differentiation strategies between *WHAT you sell* and *HOW you sell* that have been presented throughout this book. It's just one example of how you can use sales differentiation to win more deals at the prices you want. I encourage you to use the nineteen sales differentiation concepts to take your sales game to the next level.

SALES DIFFERENTIATION CONCEPTS

1. Position meaningful differentiation so buyers perceive your solution is "best"—without you saying the word.

2. Sales differentiation converts buyer intrigue into buyer action to win more deals at the prices you want.

3. Sales differentiation is not about being unique, but rather being different, relative to other buyer options.

4. Buyers will pay more for differentiated solutions that they perceive offer meaningful value.

5. Price is the ultimate decision factor in the absence of differentiation.

6. Not all differentiators matter to all Decision Influencers or in all circumstances.

7. Sales differentiation requires the salesperson to position why it matters to the buyer.

8. The ownership of a buyer perceiving differentiation resides with you, the salesperson.

9. *HOW you sell*, not just *WHAT you sell*, differentiates you.

10. Sales differentiation is not limited by product attributes, but rather by the solutions that can be innovated to address buyer challenges.

11. A Sales Crime Theory differentiates you by answering this question: *Why should this buyer want to talk with you right now?*

12. The words salespeople use, and do not use, differentiate them.

13. It's not what salespeople *say* to buyers, but rather what they *ask* of buyers, that differentiates them from the competition.

14. Sales differentiation affords you the opportunity to shape buyer decision criteria.

15. Sales differentiation enables buying process disruption.

16. Differentiate yourself by addressing buyer concerns before they arise.

17. The request for references is your last chance to differentiate with a buyer. Don't miss it.

18. Sales differentiation is a moment in time, not a permanent state.

19. The irrefutable differentiator is *YOU* . . . make it invaluable!

If you are intrigued by sales differentiation and want my help in developing your strategy, visit www.SalesDifferentiation.com. On that website, you will learn about the programs I offer and the fantastic results that participants have experienced from them.

As a result of those programs, I put together your Sales Differentiation Playbook and help indoctrinate the team with your strategy. Contact me at 763.416.4321 or Lsalz@SalesArchitects.com.

INDEX

ABOUT THE AUTHOR

Lee B. Salz is a leading sales management strategist and CEO of Sales Architects®. A recognized expert in sales differentiation, he works with senior executives and business owners across all industries helping their salespeople win more deals at the prices they want.

Lee is a frequently sought-after keynote speaker and consultant on sales differentiation, sales force development, hiring, onboarding, compensation, and other sales performance topics. He's also an award-winning author of several books including *Hire Right, Higher Profits*, the #1 rated sales management book on Amazon for 2014.

A featured columnist in *The Business Journals* and a media source on sales and sales management, Lee has been quoted and featured in *The Wall Street Journal*, CNN, *The New York Times*, MSNBC, ABC News, and numerous other outlets.

In addition to Sales Architects, Lee created The Revenue Accelerator®, a sales onboarding and enablement technology firm that structures and automates the onboarding experience for salespeople. His entrepreneurial background gives him a unique insight into the challenges executives face during growth phases.

Originally from New York and New Jersey, Lee spent ten years in the Washington, D.C. Metro area and now lives in Minneapolis with his wife, three children, and two dogs.

Lee is a championship powerlifter and a graduate of Binghamton University. When he isn't helping his clients with sales force development, you can find him on the baseball field coaching his kids.